D0931383

CAMPAIGN MEDALS OF THE BRITISH ARMY 1815-1972

CAMPAIGN MEDALS OF THE BRITISH ARMY 1815-1972

BY ROBERT W. GOULD

ARMS AND ARMOUR PRESS

Published by
Arms and Armour Press
Lionel Leventhal Limited

Great Britain
2–6 Hampstead High Street
London NW3 1QQ

Australia
4–12 Tattersalls Lane
Melbourne, Victoria 3000

United States of America
Cameron and Kelker Streets
P.O. Box 1831, Harrisburg
Pa. 17105

Canada
Fortress Publications Inc.
P.O. Box 241, Stoney Creek
Ontario 18G 3X9

ISBN 0 85368 515 0

First edition 1972
Second edition, with Price Guide Supplement, 1982

ACKNOWLEDGMENTS
The majority of the medals illustrated in
this book were loaned by Mr. Donald
Hall and the remainder by Mr. Ronald
Barden of Messrs. A. H. Baldwin & Sons
Ltd., and Mr. J. B. Hayward of Messrs. J. B.
Hayward & Son. Photography by Mr. D. J.
Teague. My grateful thanks to all four for
their co-operation, advice and, in the case
of my photographer, patience.

Printed in Great Britain
by Fakenham Press Limited
Fakenham, Norfolk

Contents

Introduction

Naval and military medallions awarded to officers have been known in this country since the reign of Queen Elizabeth I, but the first distinction which could be won by an ordinary soldier was authorised in May 1643 by Charles I. This was an oval silver badge to be worn on the breast by those who distinguished themselves in 'forlorn hopes' and was obviously a reward for gallantry. The first award for war service was a medal issued by the Commonwealth to commemorate the Battle of Dunbar, where the Royalist Scots were defeated on 3rd September 1650. This medal, gold for officers and silver for men, was worn suspended by a chain or cord from the recipient's neck. In the early nineteenth century, gold crosses and medals were awarded to senior or commanding officers for services during the Peninsular campaign of the Napoleonic Wars, but it was not until 1815 that the battle of Waterloo gave birth to the modern campaign medal—that is to say a similar medal awarded to all classes and ranks, from duke to drummer boy.

'Clasp' or 'bar' is used impartially to describe a bar which bears the name or date of a campaign or action. Although clasps were first issued with the Sutlej Campaign Medal, their origin was due to the large number of battles and engagements commemorated by the Naval and Military General Service Medals, which would otherwise have necessitated the issue of dozens of separate awards. In most cases the bar is affixed by ears to the medal suspender, but occasionally it is sewn direct onto the ribbon, as, for example, with the World War II campaign stars.

Where the medal is not described as bronze or cupro-nickel it is silver. The diameter of a medal, unless otherwise stated, it always 1.42 in (35mm) and the ribbon, with a similar proviso, is 1.25in (or 32mm). Widths of colour on the various ribbons are measured in fractions of an inch, or the metric scale, whichever is the more convenient. 10mm for example, reads very awkwardly when translated into 25/64ths of an inch. Where description of the suspender is omitted, it means that suspension is by means of a plain, straight suspender pinned through a claw to the top of the medal. This suspender usually swivels, but is occasionally fixed. The 1939-45 War Medal has a typical example of a plain, straight, non-swivelling suspender.

The obverse is the face of a medal mentioned first in any catalogue and is the side which usually bears the Sovereign's head. The reverse is the side carrying the design, and often an inscription, and cannot be seen when the medal is worn.

Order of wearing for campaign medals is in chronological sequence, but according to the date of the campaign and not the issue of the medal. For example, the holder of the India General Service Medal (1908) with bar 'Waziristan 1919-21' would wear it after any awards for World War I. Until the middle of the nineteenth century there were no instructions for precedence or manner of wearing medals, and any number of permutations appear in contemporary prints, including at least one where the holder of four medals wore them on the left side of his chest, but one up, one down and one each right and left, presumably to present a balanced effect! A later regulation laid down that medals must be worn in one or two horizontal rows and it is not uncommon to find photographs of Crimea War veterans wearing their awards in this manner; five or six medals in two rows. The custom of wearing a small piece of ribbon without the medal when in undress uniform appears to have started in India about the middle of the nineteenth century. One of the most popular misconceptions about medals appears to have originated in the early stages of World War I and is the widely held belief that a son may wear his father's medals.

Contemporary spelling has been used throughout; thus Cabul or Cabool in 1842 becomes Kabul in 1880, and Coomassie in 1874 is spelled Kumassi twenty-six years later. Early translations of Indian place names vary considerably and Bhurtphore, for instance, may also be written Burtpoor, Bhurtpoor, Burtpore, or Bhurtpore, according to taste!

Where to buy medals

Every medal collector is asked at some time or another, two questions. Why do you collect medals and where do you find them? The first answer you know, otherwise you would be browsing over the collection of vintage motor cars or matchbox labels (depending on taste and/or pocket) instead of reading this book. The answer to the second question however, tends to vary. According to some collectors, during their summer holiday they have bought for a small sum rare medals casually thrown in a box/heap/tray in a dirty junk shop situated in the back street of some seaside town. Beware these delightful tales because if only half of them are true, at certain times of the year the coast resorts are full of collectors waving aloft their valuable acquisitions and yelling 'Eureka', or whatever one shouts in these circumstances. Occasionally the venue is altered to some far-flung place but the end product is always the same—something for next to nothing.

Having scoured the back streets of many towns, the only medals I saw in junk shops were usually junk and the only medal ever offered to me in the far-flung (Northern Nigeria to be precise) was such an exorbitant price that it aggravated my prickly heat. In days of old when medals were melted down for their silver content and bronze medals were thrown on the scrap heap, there were certainly some cheap buys to be made, but not for the last ten or twenty years. Look for bargains by all means but bear in mind that many medals in junk and antique shops can be bought cheaper, and in better condition, from a reputable numismatic dealer. It is unfortunate that many collectors, especially novices, fight shy of the leading dealers. Whilst it is true that they will not give you something for nothing, certainly they will give you value for money, and if it subsequently transpires that the piece is 'wrong' your purchase money will be refunded. Small collectors grow into big collectors, and beginners with only a small amount of money to spend (a condition that afflicts most collectors from time to time) should not be deterred by an imposing address. Listed below in alphabetical order, are nine well known dealers, but this does not imply that other dealers in this country or overseas are less reputable or reliable.

A.H. Baldwin & Sons Ltd., 11 Adelphi Terrace, London W.C.2 N66J.

Forman Medals & Militaria Ltd., Stratford House, St. Peter's Place, Broad Street, Birmingham B.1.

Donald Hall, 23 Denmark Street, London WC2H 8NA.

P. Hinkla, 226 East 89th Street, New York, NY 10028, U.S.A.

J.B. Hayward & Son, 17 Piccadilly Arcade,

London S.W.1.

Alec Kaplan & Son (PTY) Ltd., P.O. Box 132, Germiston, Transvaal, South Africa.

Charles A. Lusted, 96a Calverley Road, Tunbridge Wells, Kent.

B.A. Seaby Ltd., 59-65, Great Portland Street, London W.1.

Spink & Son Ltd., 5-7 King Street, St. James's, London S.W.1

Classification and condition

Whilst the condition of a medal is sometimes a matter of opinion (buyers and sellers tend to have differing views) it's worth, as with all collectable material, varies according to the rarity of the piece. To put it plainly, a knocked about World War I Victory Medal may not be given house room, whereas a fifteen bar Military General Service Medal with similar damage would be received with open arms. A realistic guide to condition reads something like this: Mint, should mean what it says, pristine condition; E.F., extremely fine, small scuff marks and minute flaws; V.F., very fine, obvious signs of wear and tear, possibly marked by contact with other medals, but no major defects; F. fine, but not fine as applied to a fine piece of porcelain but rather well worn; Fair, means fairly well battered and if some honest citizen puts Worn as a description, it may well be difficult to determine whether the item started life as a medal or a crown piece. Any permutation is possible and a medal is sometimes described as VF/EF, meaning that the obverse (always given first) is only V.F. whilst the reverse is extremely fine. Occasionally one sees classifications such as N.E.F., meaning nearly E.F., or G.V.F. for Good Very Fine, i.e., better than V.F. but not good enough for E.F., as an attempt to give a more precise definition. In this context, the description of a medal shown as 'E.F. apart from two edge knocks' is rather like writing 'Motor car, as new, apart from two crumpled mudguards'. Similarly, an invitation to buy a medal which is 'E.F. (but once converted to a menu holder)' is similar to 'Pair of valuable short swords (have been adapted as coal tongs)'. It is a good working rule to avoid like the plague any medal which has been renamed, repaired or rehashed in any way unless it is sold for little more than the value of the silver content.

Research

Once the bug has bitten, the collector often wishes to find out something about the man, probably long since dead, whose medals he now holds. The best course is the Public Record Office, Chancery Lane, London, W.C.2., which houses medal rolls, muster rolls, description books, service documents and discharges; followed by the India Office Library and Records, Orbit House, Blackfriars Road, London, S.E.1., and curators of regimental museums. The latter are usually run on a tight budget so please remember to enclose a stamped, addressed envelope. Bear in mind, however, that records are often incomplete, parts having been lost or destroyed and the quest is further complicated by human errors which have crept into these documents. For example, there is no record of service of either Captain Marschatik who appears in the Waterloo Medal Roll or Captain Marschalek who was eligible for the Military General Service Medal. They were in fact the same man, Captain Gustavus von Marschalk, which is the name shown in the Army list; but on his half-pay papers, signed by the man himself, the spelling is 'Marschalck'.

As with all detective work, the end product of research is often frustrating, sometimes sublime and occasionally ridiculous. I once spent two days wading through documents to find why a cavalryman, whose Military General Service Medal is in my possession, had been pensioned. Amid a welter of papers of men wounded by musket balls, riddled by grapeshot and slashed by swords, what terrible wound had struck down my hussar trumpeter? According to his discharge papers he 'suffered a diseased testicle as the result of a fall from his horse at Menin in 1815'. So much for the thundering hooves and flashing sabres!

As a novice I was somewhat overawed by people who suggested quite elaborate methods of card indexing a collection, writing it up, display cases and so forth. It all sounded very complicated and a far cry from just collecting a few medals. It is, of course, a matter for the individual; a collection can be housed with special lighting, descriptive cards, etc., or, at the other extreme, it can be tumbled into the odd drawer or shoe box. The last method is certainly guaranteed not to improve the condition of any medal, but on the other hand I have seen equally cavalier treatment by people who are presumed to know better. Certainly the average collector will wish to keep a notebook in which to record the price and date of purchase of his medals, if nothing else.

To clean or not to clean is purely a matter of personal preference. If one collector prefers his medals looking aged and suspended from old

Display and cleaning

ribbons, as opposed to the man who likes shining bright awards with new ribbons, who is to say which of them is wrong? Certainly not me.

Never commit the cardinal sin of splitting a named group to take out one or two medals for the collection—you will not only throw away history but also money. Far better to sell the group intact and use the money to buy the odd medal to make a set.

The following list is arranged alphabetically by towns and is merely a guide to places where campaign medals are on view to the public. The visiting hours may vary considerably between summer and winter, and there are a large number of museums who admit visitors by appointment only at weekends.

Where to see British campaign medals

Before making a long journey it is therefore wise to verify times with the curator or custodian by letter. It must be stressed that this list is not comprehensive and is generally limited to museums visited by the author. There are a few surprising omissions and one is the Royal Maritime Museum at Greenwich, where the magnificent displays completely overshadow a small case of medals, not written up, tucked away in a corner. Similarly, the medal room at the Imperial War Musem, Lambeth, caters chiefly for awards and medals issued as the result of both World Wars. Finally, I apologise in advance to curators who display medals in their museums which are not mentioned.

ASH VALE, near Aldershot, Hampshire. Royal Army Medical Corps, Keogh Barracks. Excellent display, includes a photograph of Surgeon Manley's decorations; the only man to wear both the V.C. and Iron Cross.
BEVERLEY, Yorkshire, 11 Butcher Row. Prince of Wales' Own Regiment of Yorkshire.
BLANDFORD FORUM, Blandford Camp, Dorset, Royal Signals.
CANTERBURY, Kent, Stour Street. The Buffs. Room devoted to medals, including many interesting groups.
CARLISLE, Cumberland, The Keep, The Castle. The Border Regiment.
CHATHAM, Kent. Brompton Barracks. Royal Engineers.
CHICHESTER, Sussex. Chichester City Museum, 29 Little London. (Closed weekends).

DORCHESTER, Dorset, The Keep,. Dorset
Regiment and the Devonshire &
Dorset Regiment as well as local
yeomanry and militia. Nearly 1,500
medals on display.
HALIFAX, Yorkshire, Bankfield Museum, Haley
Hill. Duke of Wellington's Regiment
and 4th/7th Royal Dragoon Guards.
LANCASTER, Lancashire, Old Town Hall, Market
Square. King's Own Royal Regiment.
LICHFIELD, Staffordshire, Whittington Barracks.
Staffordshire Regiment.
LINCOLN, Lincolnshire, Sobraon Barracks,
Burton Road. Royal Lincolnshire
Regiment.
LONDON, S.W.3., Royal Hospital, Chelsea.
National Army Museum.
LONDON, E.C.3., H.M. Tower of London. The
Royal Fusiliers.
MAIDSTONE, Kent, Maidstone Museum, St. Faith
Street. Queen's Own Royal West
Kents.
NORTHAMPTON, Northamptonshire, Gibraltar
Barracks, Barrack Road.
Northamptonshire Regiment.
NOTTINGHAM, Nottinghamshire, The Castle.
Notts & Derby Regiment. Interesting
display includes a campaign medal
awarded to a goat.
RICHMOND, Yorkshire, Gallowgate. The Green
Howards. Over 2,000 medals dis-
played.
SHEFFIELD, Yorkshire, Endcliffe Hall, Endcliffe
Vale Road. The York and Lancaster
Regiment. Outstanding collection of
medals.
SHREWSBURY, Shropshire, Clive House, College
Hill. 1st King's Dragoon Guards and
The Bays.
SOUTHSEA, Sussex, R.M. Barracks, Eastney. The
Royal Marines. (Do not believe stories
by former 'royals' that the museum
displays a Waterloo medal to a Royal
Marine—it doesn't).
TAUNTON, Somerset, 14 Mount Street. Somerset
Light Infantry. Excellent medal
gallery.
WARRINGTON, Lancashire, Peninsula Barracks.
East and South Lancs. Regiments.
WARWICK, Warwickshire, The Lord Leycester
Hospital, High Street. 3rd King's Own
and 7th Queen's Own Hussars.
WARWICK, St. John's House. The Royal

Warwicks. Large collection of medals.

WINCHESTER, Hampshire, Peninsular Barracks.
The Royal Green Jackets. An outstanding display of medals including a
Naval General Service medal to the
95th and several unique groups.

WINCHESTER, Serles House, Southgate Street.
The Royal Hampshires. Some interesting 'long' groups.

ABERDEEN, Scotland, St. Lukes, Viewfield
Road. The Gordon Highlanders.

EDINBURGH, Scotland, Crown Square, The
Castle. Scottish United Services
Museum. Well worth a visit for anyone
interested in any aspect of militaria or
military history.

FORT GEORGE, Scotland. Seaforth Highlanders
and the Queen's Own Cameron
Highlanders.

GLASGOW, Scotland, 518 Sauchiehall Street.
Royal Highland Fusiliers.

HAMILTON, Scotland, 129 Muir Street. The
Cameronians.

PERTH, Scotland, Balhousie Castle. The Black
Watch.

STIRLING, Scotland, The Castle. The Argyll &
Sutherland Highlanders.

BRECON, Wales, The Barracks. The South Wales
Borderers and Monmouthshire
Regiment. Separate medal room with
exhibits dating back to eighteenth
century.

CAERNARVON, Wales, The Queen's Tower,
Caernarvon Castle. The Royal Welsh
Fusiliers.

ARMAGH, N. Ireland, Sovereign's House, The
Mall. The Royal Irish Fusiliers.

Where to meet other collectors

Every collector benefits by contact with kindred souls, whether it be exchange of information, swopping duplicates, or just chatting about aspects of the hobby. The largest society in this country is The Orders and Medals Research Society whose Hon. General Secretary is N.G. Gooding, 11 Mares Field, Chepstow Road, Croydon CRO 5UA. In addition to holding London meetings, the Society also publishes a hefty quarterly journal, packed with information and well worth the subscription fee. A fairly comprehensive library is also available to members. The other society which caters solely for medal collectors is The Birmingham Medal Society, Hon. Secretary, M.F. Minton, 50 All Saints Road, King's Heath, Birmingham 14.

Some of the other societies in English Speaking countries are as follows: Orders and Medals Society of America (librarian W.P. Huber), 1742 W. Henderson Street, Chicago 13, Illinois, U.S.A.; Military Collectors Club of Canada (secretary Captain J. Boddington) 8828 160th Street, Edmonton 52, Alberta, Canada; the South African Numismatic Society (secretary Dr. Frank Mitchell J.C.D.,E.S.A.N.S.), P.O. Box 1073, Capetown, South Africa; Military Historical Society of Ireland, whose secretary's address is 48, Sweetmount Park, Dundrum Heights, Dublin 14, Eire. Societies in Australia are organized on a state, rather than national, basis.

Bibliography

Carter, Thomas, 'Medals of the British Army and how they were won', London. Revised edition 1893. Reprinted London, 1972, as 'War Medals of the British Army 1650-1891.' Fair amount of detail on actions and units, especially in the Crimea War.

Dorling, Captain H. Taprell, in association with L.F. Guille, 'Ribbons and Medals', London. Last edition 1965. Very wide coverage of British and foreign awards.

Gordon, Major L.L., 'British Battles and Medals', Aldershot. 4th edition 1971. Excellent book on campaign medals, including units engaged, but do not be alarmed if the particular regiment you seek is not shown.

Irwin, D. Hastings., 'War Medals and Decorations', London. 4th edition 1910. An informative book both for the beginner and general collector.

Long, W.H., 'Medals of the British Navy and how they were won', London, 1895. Probably the best book on naval medals, with great detail of actions, ships engaged and naval landing brigades.

Purves, Alec A., 'Collecting Medals and Decorations', London, 1968. Excellent value for money and contains useful advice and information not readily found elsewhere.

Steward, W. Augustus, 'War Medals and Their History', London, 1915. A useful book containing a fair amount of information.

1. Waterloo Medal. 18th June 1815

The Battle of Waterloo, which changed the course of history and gave employment to numerous authors, publishers and camera-men, was also responsible for a silver medal–a medal with three distinctions. It was the first medal to be awarded by the British Crown to all its troops irrespective of rank, the first campaign medal to be given to the next-of-kin of men killed in action and the first medal to have the recipient's name impressed by a machine. Although named the Waterloo medal it was actually awarded, at the suggestion of the Duke of Wellington, for Quatre Bras on the 16th, the fighting on the 17th and Waterloo proper on the 18th. Every British and King's German Legion soldier present at these actions was credited with two years' extra service to count for pay, promotion and pension.

This medal, 1.4in in diameter, was instituted by an order dated 10th March 1816 and a later instruction was issued that the ribbon was never to be worn without the medal. The Waterloo veterans, justly proud of their award, promptly wore the medal in all weathers and, if contemporary accounts are true, many of the discharged rank and file often wore it with civilian clothes. As a result, the steel ring through which the ribbon was threaded often rusted and many recipients replaced the ring with some form of silver suspension of their own design. For the Peninsular veterans these suspenders were

sometimes engraved, or carried unofficial clasps, bearing the names of previous battles and actions. Since the ribbon was normally sewn on the jacket some officers provided themselves with duplicates (one for each uniform) which were usually other ranks' medals with the original recipient's particulars erased. A copy of the Waterloo medal also made an appear-ance, slightly smaller and thinner than the official award and omitting the designer's name. This was possibly made for a similar reason or, as depicted in prints of the period, to allow a wife to wear a replica of her husband's medal on gala occasions.

On the obverse of the medal, designed by T. Wyon, is the laureated head of the Prince Regent and the legend GEORGE P. REGENT. The nicely balanced reverse depicts the Grecian winged figure of Victory, seated on a pedestal, holding a palm branch in her right hand and an olive branch in her left. Above her head is the word WELLINGTON and in a rectangle, below the pedestal, the word WATER-LOO. Beneath the rectangle is the date JUNE 18 1815 in two lines. The ribbon is crimson with quarter-inch wide dark blue edges. The individual naming is in large impressed capitals and always includes the regiment or unit; the blank spaces at either end are usually filled by two or three stars. Suspension is by means of a steel clip, sweated to the top of the medal, through which passed a steel ring 1.1in in diameter.

2. Military General Service Medal 1793–1814

A medal for twenty-one years war service, but with bars which cover only thirteen of those years; authorised forty-six years after the first campaign it commemorates; issued fifty-five years after the first date on the medal and then only to survivors and, finally, bearing the head of a sovereign not even born when some of the earlier engagements were fought–such is the 'Dead Man's Medal'. Although the survivors of 1815 proudly wore their Waterloo medals, the veterans of the other battles of the Napoleonic Wars had nothing to show for their services, except scars, despite efforts made on their behalf by the Duke of Richmond. However, not until a medal for the Scinde Wars of 1843 was granted by the British Government did mounting public opinion overcome the opposition of the Duke of Wellington (and probably the Exchequer). A silver medal was finally instituted in 1847, together with twenty-eight clasps covering actions between 1806 and 1814; then in 1850 a further Order authorised a clasp for Egypt, 1801.

The twenty-nine bars finally authorised were as follows:
EGYPT (2nd March to 2nd September 1801) MAIDA (4th July 1806) ROLEIA (17th August 1808) VIMIERA (21st August 1808) SAHAGUN (21st December 1808) BENEVENTE (29th December 1808) SAHAGUN AND BENEVENTE (Awarded to those present at both actions) CORUNNA (16th January 1809) MARTINIQUE (30th January to 24th February 1809) TALAVERA (27th and 28th July 1809) GUADALOUPE (January and February 1810) BUSACO (27th September 1810) BARROSA (5th March 1811) FUENTES D'ONOR (5th May 1811) ALBUHERA (16th May 1811) JAVA (10th to 26th August 1811) CIUDAD RODRIGO (8th to 19th January 1812) BADAJOZ (17th March to 6th April 1812) SALAMANCA (22nd July 1812) FORT DETROIT (August 1812) VITTORIA (21st June 1813) PYRENEES (25th July to 2nd August 1813) ST. SEBASTIAN (17th July to 8th September 1813) CHATEAUGUAY (26th October 1813) NIVELLE (10th November 1813) CHRYSTLER'S FARM (11th November 1813) NIVE (9th to 13th December 1813) ORTHES (27th Feburary 1814) TOULOUSE (10th April 1814).

The first date on the medal seems to indicate that clasps for earlier actions were contemplated, possibly Lincelles or Nieuport in Flanders, in August and October 1793 respectively. In any case, there are some surprising omissions from

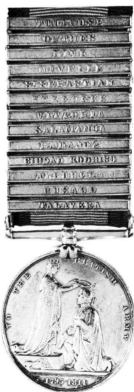

the final lists of clasps, namely the capture of the Cape of Good Hope from the Dutch in 1806 with the loss of only 16 killed and 137 wounded and the brilliant victory at Kioge, outside Copenhagen, in the following year. Prisoners, guns, stores, sixty-four ships of the Danish Fleet, the Island of Heligoland and nearly £1,000,000 in prize money—all this for total British casualties of 43 killed and 145 wounded. The cavalry action at Sahagun (2 killed and 18 wounded) earned a clasp; but not so Wellington's first victory in the Peninsula, the passage of the Douro where there were 119 casualties. The capture of Guadaloupe in 1810 (273 casualties) merited a bar, but not the taking of St. Lucia in 1796 with 405 men dead and wounded. Similar examples could be repeated indefinitely, but it is strange that all these engagements won battle honours for the units engaged, but not battle clasps. Nearly 26,000 medals were issued, a surprising number considering the passage of time, bearing between them about 84,000 clasps. The number of clasps per medal ranged from fifteen awarded to two recipients, to over

eight thousand with only one. Whilst the double figure clasps are most impressive, some of the medals with fewer bars show an amazing range of service and years. Richard Wittle's ten years with the 90th Foot, for example, only earned him three clasps but he ranged as far afield as Egypt, Martinique and Guadaloupe.

On the obverse of the medal is the diademed head of Queen Victoria with the legend VICTORIA REGINA and the date 1848. The reverse shows the young Queen standing on a dais about to place a laurel wreath on the head of the Duke of Wellington, who is kneeling before her and holding his Field Marshal's Baton. Beside the dais is a small British Lion dormant and in the exergue below are the dates 1793-1814. Following the curve of the upper half circle of the medal is the inscription TO THE BRITISH ARMY. It was designed by W. Wyon and the ribbon is crimson with eight-of-an-inch wide dark blue borders. The individual naming is in large, impressed capitals and the rank, name and unit is always shown. The medal was never issued without a bar.

3.   Naval General Service Medal 1793—1840

In common with the victories of their military brethren, the brilliant successes of the officers and men of the Royal Navy during the Napoleonic Wars went unrecognized until a General Order dated 1st June 1847 authorised the striking of a medal to cover the years 1793 to 1815. A later Order extended the qualifying dates to include the fleet actions at Algiers in 1816, Navarino in 1827 and the coast of Syria in 1840. A total of 231 were authorised which not only covered famous battles such as Camperdown, Nile, Trafalgar, and so on, but also a large number of single ship and cutting-out actions. However, after a lapse of so many years, it is perhaps not surprising that only about 21,000 medals were actually claimed and there were no claimants for several of the bars. The medal was never issued without a bar and a total of about 24,000 bars were awarded; but nearly 10,000 of these commemorated the three later battles fought between 1816 and 1840.

The maximum number of bars issued with any one medal was seven and there were two such medals, both to officers. In common with other campaign medals only the recipients knew the true worth of the award. During the battle of the Glorious First of June, a son was born to a Mrs. McKenzie on board H.M.S. TREMENDOUS; fifty-four years later Daniel Tremendous McKenzie duly

received his medal with the bar 1ST JUNE 1794, awarded for a battle on the day he was born. The fourteen claimants who had served on H.M.S. AGINCOURT, a 64gun ship of the line, no doubt received their medals with pride, despite the fact that their captain was court-martialled after the battle for failing to bring his ship into close action. On the other hand, it appears that many of the veterans did not receive the full tally of bars to which they were entitled.

In the following list of bars, the dates in brackets for fleet and ship actions are given for reference—the dates do not appear on the actual clasps. The abbreviation WH on bars indicates 'with' and BOAT SERVICE commemorates numerous 'cutting-out' and similar engagements by crews of ships' boats.

15 MARCH BOAT SERVICE 1793
NYMPHE 18th JUNE 1793
CRESCENT 20 OCTR. 1793
ZEBRA 17 MARCH 1794
17 MAR. BOAT SERVICE 1794
CARYSFORT 29 MAY 1794
1 JUNE 1794
ROMNEY 17 JUNE 1794
BLANCHE 4 JANY. 1795
LIVELY 13 MARCH 1795
14 MARCH 1795
ASTRAEA 10 APRIL 1795
THETIS 17 MAY 1795
HUSSAR 17 MAY 1795

MOSQUITO 9 JUNE 1795
17 JUNE 1795
23rd JUNE 1795
DIDO 24 JUNE 1795
LOWESTOFFE 24 JUNE 1795
SPIDER 25 AUGT. 1795
PORT SPERGUI (17 March 1796)
INDEFATIGABLE 20 APL. 1796
UNICORN 8 JUNE 1796
STA. MARGARITTA 8 JUNE 1796
SOUTHAMPTON 9 JUNE 1796
DRYAD 13 JUNE 1796
TERPSICHORE 13 OCTR. 1796
LAPWING 3 DECR. 1796
MINERVE 19 DECR. 1796
BLANCHE 19 DEC. 1796
INDEFATIGABLE 13 JANY. 1797
AMAZON 13 JANY. 1797
ST. VINCENT (14th February 1797)
SAN FIORENZO 8 MARCH 1797
NYMPHE 8 MARCH 1797
29 MAY BOAT SERVICE 1797
CAMPERDOWN (11th October 1797)
PHOEBE 21 DECR. 1797
MARS 21 APRIL 1798
ISLE ST. MARCOU (6 May 1798)
LION 15 JULY 1798
NILE (1st August 1798)
ESPOIR 7 AUGT. 1798
12th OCTOBER 1798
FISGARD 20 OCTR. 1798
SYBILLE 28 FEBY. 1799
TELEGRAPH 18 MARCH 1799
ACRE (20 May 1799)
9 JUNE BOAT SERVICE 1799

SCHIERMONNIKOOG 12 AUGT. 1799
ARROW 13 SEPT. 1799
WOLVERINE 13 SEPT. 1799
SURPRISE WITH HERMIONE (25th
October 1799)
SPEEDY 6 NOVR. 1799
COURIER 23 NOVR. 1799
20 DEC. BOAT SERVICE 1799
VIPER 26 DECR. 1799
FAIRY 5 FEB. 1800
HARPY 5 FEBY. 1800
PETEREL 21 MARCH 1800
PENELOPE 30 MARCH 1800
VINCIEGO 30 MARCH 1800
CAPTURE OF THE DESIREE (8th July
1800)
29 JULY BOAT SERVICE 1800
SEINE 20 AUGT. 1800
29 AUG. BOAT SERVICE 1800
27 OCT. BOAT SERVICE 1800
PHOEBE 19 FEBY. 1801
EGYPT (March-September 1801)
COPENHAGEN 1801 (2 April 1801)
SPEEDY 6 MAY 1801
GUT OF GIBRALTAR 12 JULY 1801
21 JULY BOAT SERVICE 1801
SYLPH 28 SEPTR. 1801
PASLEY 28 OCTR. 1801
27 JUNE BOAT SERVICE 1803
4 NOV. BOAT SERVICE 1803
4 FEB. BOAT SERVICE 1804
SCORPION 31 MARCH 1804
BEAVER 31 MARCH 1804
CENTURION 18 SEPT. 1804
ARROW 3 FEBY. 1805

ACHERON 3 FEBY. 1805
SAN FIORENZO 14 FEBY. 1805
4 JUNE BOAT SERVICE 1805
PHOENIX 10 AUGT. 1805
TRAFALGAR (21st October 1805)
4 NOVR. 1805
ST. DOMINGO (6th February 1806)
LONDON 13 MARCH 1806
AMAZON 13 MARCH 1806
PIQUE 26 MARCH 1806
SIRIUS 17 APRIL 1806
16 JULY BOAT SERVICE 1806
BLANCHE 19 JULY 1806
ARETHUSA 23 AUGT. 1806
ANSON 23 AUGT. 1806
CURACOA 1 JANY. 1807
2 JAN. BOAT SERVICE 1807
PICKLE 3 JANY. 1807
21 JAN. BOAT SERVICE 1807
19 APL. BOAT SERVICE 1807
HYDRA 6 AUGT. 1807
COMUS 15 AUGT. 1807
LOUISA 28 OCTR. 1807
CARRIER 14 NOVR. 1807
ANN 24 NOVR. 1807
13 FEB. BOAT SERVICE 1808
SAPPHO 2 MARCH 1808
SAN FIORENZO 8 MARCH 1808
EMERALD 13 MARCH 1808
CHILDERS 14 MARCH 1808
STATELY 22 MARCH 1808
NASSAU 22 MARCH 1808
OFF ROTA 4 APRIL 1808
GRASSHOPPER 24 APRIL 1808
RAPID 24 APRIL 1808
REDWING 7 MAY 1808
VIRGINIE 19 MAY 1808
REDWING 31 MAY 1808
SEAHORSE WH. BADERE ZAFFER (6th
July 1808)
10 JULY BOAT SERVICE 1808
COMET 11 AUGT. 1808
11 AUG. BOAT SERVICE 1808
CENTAUR 26 AUGT. 1808
IMPLACABLE 26 AUGT. 1808
CRUIZER 1 NOVR. 1808
AMETHYST WH. THETIS (10th
November 1808)
28 NOV. BOAT SERVICE 1808
OFF THE PEARL ROCK 13 DECR. 1808
ONYX 1 JANY. 1809
CONFIANCE 14 JANY. 1809
MARTINIQUE (February 1809)
HORATIO 10 FEBY. 1809
SUPERIEURE 10 FEBY. 1809
AMETHYST 5 APRIL 1809
BASQUE ROADS 1809 (12th April)
POMPEE 17 JUNE 1809
CASTOR 17 JUNE 1809
RECRUIT 17 JUNE 1809
CYANE 25-27 JUNE 1809
L'ESPOIR 25-27 JUNE 1809
BONNE CITOYENNE WH. FURIEUSE
(6th July 1809)
7 JULY BOAT SERVICE 1809
14 JULY BOAT SERVICE 1809

25 JULY BOAT SERVICE 1809
27 JULY BOAT SERVICE 1809
29 JULY BOAT SERVICE 1809
28 AUG. BOAT SERVICE 1809
DIANA 11 SEPT. 1809
1 NOV. BOAT SERVICE 1809
13 DEC. BOAT SERVICE 1809
ANSE LA BARQUE 18 DECR. 1809
CHEROKEE 10 JANY. 1810
SCORPION 12 JANY. 1810
GUADALOUPE (January-February
1810)
THISTLE 10 FEBY. 1810
13 FEB. BOAT SERVICE 1810
SURLY 24 APRIL 1810
FIRM 24 APRIL 1810
SYLVIA 26 APRIL 1810
1 MAY BOAT SERVICE 1810
SPARTAN 3 MAY 1810
ROYALIST MAY & JUNE 1810
28 JUNE BOAT SERVICE 1810
AMANTHEA 25 JULY 1810
BANDA NEIRA (9th August 1810)
BOADICEA 18 SEPT. 1810
OTTER 18 SEPT. 1810
STAUNCH 18 SEPT. 1810
27 SEPT. BOAT SERVICE 1810
BRISEIS 14 OCTR. 1810
4 NOV. BOAT SERVICE 1810
23 NOV. BOAT SERVICE 1810
24 DEC. BOAT SERVICE 1810
LISSA (13th March 1811)
ANHOLT 27 MARCH 1811
ARROW 6 APRIL 1811
4 MAY BOAT SERVICE 1811
OFF TAMATAVE 20 MAY 1811
30 JULY BOAT SERVICE 1811
2 AUG. BOAT SERVICE 1811
HAWKE 18 AUGT. 1811
JAVA (August-September 1811)
20 SEPT. BOAT SERVICE 1811
SKYLARK 11 NOVR. 1811
LOCUST 11 NOVR. 1811
PELAGOSA 29 NOVR. 1811
4 DEC. BOAT SERVICE 1811
VICTORIOUS WH. RIVOLI (22nd
February 1812)
WEASEL 22 FEBY. 1812
ROSARIO 27 MARCH 1812
GRIFFON 27 MARCH 1812
4 APL. BOAT SERVICE 1812
NORTHUMBERLAND 22 MAY 1812
GROWLER 22 MAY 1812
MALAGA 29 MAY 1812
OFF MARDOE 6 JULY 1812
SEALARK 21 JULY 1812
1 SEPT. BOAT SERVICE 1812
17 SEPT. BOAT SERVICE 1812
29 SEPT. BOAT SERVICE 1812
ROYALIST 29 DECR. 1812
6 JANY. BOAT SERVICE 1813
21 MARCH BOAT SERVICE 1813
WEASEL 22 APRIL 1813
28 APRIL BOAT SERVICE 1813
APL. & MAY BOAT SERVICE 1813
2 MAY BOAT SERVICE 1813

20

SHANNON WH. CHESAPEAKE (1st June 1813)
PELICAN 14 AUGT. 1813
ST. SEBASTIAN (August-September 1813)
THUNDER 9 OCTR. 1813
GLUCKSTADT 5 JANY. 1814
VENERABLE 16 JANY. 1814
CYANE 16 JANY. 1814 ,
EUROTAS 25 FEBY. 1814
HEBRUS WH. L'ETOILE (27th March 1814)
PHOEBE 28 MARCH 1814
CHERUB 28 MARCH 1814
8 APL. BOAT SERVICE 1814 .
24 MAY BOAT SERVICE 1814
THE POTOMAC 17 AUGT. 1814
3 & 6 SEPT. BOAT SERVICE 1814
14 DEC. BOAT SERVICE 1814

ENDYMION WH. PRESIDENT (15th January 1815)
PILOT 17 JUNE 1815
GAIETA 24 JULY 1815
ALGIERS (27th August 1816)
NAVARINO (20th October 1827)
SYRIA (November 1840)

The obverse of the medal is similar to the Military General Service medal. The reverse shows the figure of Britannia holding a trident and seated on a seahorse. It was designed by W. Wyon and the ribbon is white with blue edges. The individual naming is indented in Roman capitals and the rank is only included if the recipient is an officer or warrant officer; the name of the ship is never given.

4.   Army of India 1799–1826

The London Gazette of 28th February 1851 carried an official notice that the Honourable East India Company had been authorised to issue a medal to all survivors of the forces who had seen active service in India between 1799 and 1826. However, active service and disease in India, coupled with the passage of time, had left few claimants for the award. Over 40,000 men had fought in the six general actions of the First Mahratta War, for which clasps were awarded, but less than two hundred lived to claim their medals. The 1st Bengal European Regiment (later the Royal Munster Fusiliers) was over eight hundred strong the evening before the Battle of Deig, but only three of them were still alive to claim their medals in 1851. The clasp for Bhurtpore commemorated the successful attack in 1826; there was no award for the four unsuccessful attempts to storm the city in 1803, which cost over 3,000 casualties, (killed and wounded). Bhurtpore incidentally was seven miles in circumference with high mud walls, sixty feet thick, garrisoned by 20,000 men and reckoned to be impregnable. At 8 o'clock on the morning of 18th January 1826 a mine containing 10,000 pounds of black powder was exploded under one of the· walls. Amid still-falling debris and clouds of dust, the storming columns surged forward into the breach, the forlorn hope carrying a black flag to show that no quarter would be given. Such was the type of savage fighting commemorated by this medal.

Twenty-one clasps were finally authorised, as shown below, and the medal was never issued without a clasp, or unnamed. The order of the bars is different to most awards in that the last clasp is nearest the medal (in other words

the correct order reads downwards).

ALLIGHUR (4th September 1803) Storming of Fort Allighur in the First Mahratta War.

BATTLE OF DELHI (11th September 1803) Scinde Army of 20,000 defeated by Lord Lake.

ASSAYE (23rd September 1803) The first of Wellington's victories with 4,000 troops against a French officered native army of 50,000.

ASSEERGHUR (21st October 1803)
Surrender of Fort Asseerghur.

LASWARREE (1st November 1803) The
Mahratta Army marching to
recapture Delhi, defeated and
dispersed with heavy casualties.

ARGAUM (29th November 1803) Battle
on the plain of Argaum.

GAWILGHUR (15th December 1803)
Siege and assault of a fortress of
that name.

DEFENCE OF DELHI (8th-14th October
1804) Attempt by Holkar to
recapture the city.

BATTLE OF DEIG (13th November
1804) A heavily contested battle
near River Jumna.

CAPTURE OF DEIG (11th-23rd
December 1804) Siege and storming of the fortress.

NEPAUL (October 1814-March 1816) A
two year campaign against the
Gurkhas.

KIRKEE (5th November 1817) A
Mahratta army of 26,000 defeated
near Poona.

POONA (11th-16th November 1817) The
taking of Poona.

KIRKEE AND POONA. Awarded to
troops engaged in both actions.

SEETABULDEE (26th-27th November
1817) The defeat of the army of
the Rajah of Berar, near the city of
Nagpore. Although sanctioned, it is
doubtful whether this clasp was
ever actually claimed.

NAGPORE (16th December 1817) Siege
and surrender of the city of
Nagpore.

SEETABULDEE AND NAGPORE.
Awarded to troops engaged in both
actions.

MAHEIDPOOR (21st December 1817)
Battle against the Pindarries.

CORYGAUM (1st January 1818) British
column successfully defended itself
against attack by over 28,000
enemy cavalry and infantry.

AVA (1824-1826) Campaign in Burma—
the only clasp for which the Royal
Navy qualified.

BHURTPOOR (17th-18th January 1826)
See text.

Drummer Colston of the 15th and 31st
Native Infantry was the only recipient of a
medal with seven clasps, and these covered
a period of twenty-three years continuous
service in India, from Allighur in 1803 to
Bhurtpore in 1826. The medal rolls also
record that just over three hundred men
held the Army of India medal in conjunction with the Military General Service
medal, and of these twenty-three also
received the Waterloo medal.

On the reverse of the medal is the

seated figure of Victory holding a laurel
branch in her right hand and a wreath in
her left. Against a palm tree in the left
background is a trophy of arms, consisting
of Indian armour and weapons. The
inscription TO THE ARMY OF INDIA
follows the curve of the upper half circle
of the medal, while in the exergue below
are the dates 1799-1826. The obverse,
similar to plate 2, shows the diademed
head of Queen Victoria with the legend
VICTORIA REGINA. An ornate
swivelling suspender, the prototype for
many mid-Victorian campaign medals,
holds the light blue ribbon. Naming is
usually in large impressed capitals to
British regiments and engraved in running
script to Indian troops.

5. Ghuznee Medal
21st–23rd July 1839

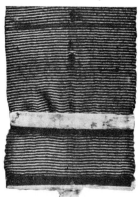

The First Afghan War proved very prolific
in honours and medals, and the storming
of the fortress of Ghuznee appears to have
set the pattern. This action earned the
commander-in-chief a peerage, field
officers and above the Order of the
Dooranee Empire, all ranks were awarded
the Ghuznee Medal and the eleven
regiments concerned were each granted a

battle honour—all this for less than 150 casualties, most of them wounded.

On the obverse of the medal is the fortress of Ghuznee with the name GHUZNEE below in a curved exergue. The reverse shows a mural crown with the date 23RD JULY above and the year 1839 below; the whole is surrounded by a laurel wreath, with a space for the recipient's name. The piece is 1.46in in diameter and the ribbon is 1.5in wide. The ribbon was originally half green, half yellow, but was changed to the present colour of half crimson and half green. Suspension is by means of a straight suspender and attachment, sweated onto the top of the medal. Apparently two separate dies were used for the obverse, as one type has a much wider border than the other. The awards were issued unnamed and consequently there is a wide variety in the styles of naming (privately executed) which may be found on the reverse or on the rim.

6. Candahar, Ghuznee and Cabul Medals October 1841 – October 1842. First Afghan War

There are four different strikings of this silver medal, which was authorised by a General Order in India in October 1842, but only one medal could be earned by any one man. This medal commemorates the somewhat confused fighting in North West India and Afghanistan with casualties which would have passed unnoticed in the wars of the twentieth century. General Nott's army for example, in the skirmish outside the fortress of Ghuznee in August 1842, had 24 killed—only two of whom were British—and earned battle honours for six regiments. It appears that the Indian Government was much more liberal with its honours than the Crown—no wonder the Peninsular veterans are reported to have been enraged.

The obverse of each medal is the same and bears the familiar diademed head of young Queen Victoria but with the legend VICTORIA VINDEX. The reverse side of each medal is as follows:

1. CANDAHAR with the date 1842 underneath, the whole surrounded by a laurel wreath and surmounted by a crown.
2. CABUL instead of CANDAHAR, otherwise similar.
3. Two entwined laurel wreaths, practically forming two circles, with GHUZNEE in the first loop and CABUL in the second. The whole is surmounted by a crown and the date 1842 appears below the wreaths.
4. The names CANDAHAR, GHUZNEE and CABUL and the date 1842 in that order, on four lines. Again, the whole is surrounded by a laurel wreath and surmounted by a crown.

The medal was designed by W. Wyon and the ribbon, 1.75in wide, is rainbow-pattern watered red, white, yellow, white and blue. There is a straight steel suspender pinned to a steel clip fastened to the medal. Some of these medals are named in script, others in indented capitals and some are unnamed.

7.   Jellalabad Medals 12th November 1841—7th April 1842. First Afghan War.

These medals commemorate the defence of Jellalabad by a small British and Indian force who not only had to contend with besieging Afghans, but also short rations, treason and a number of earthquake shocks which demolished a third of the town and some of the defences. The first medal was approved by a General Order from Allahabad dated 30th April 1842 and was minted in Calcutta. It is generally known as the 'Mural Crown' since the obverse shows a mural crown superscribed JELLALABAD and the reverse has the date VII APRIL 1842 in three lines. The siege was abandoned on this date after a determined attack by the besieged on the Afghan lines. This medal may be found with either a straight steel suspender fitted directly to the rim of the piece, or held by a ring fitted to the medal. The style of naming varies considerably and, in addition, may be named on the edge or on the obverse under the crown. It appears, therefore, that the medal was originally issued unnamed.

The appearance of the second medal, generally referred to as 'Flying Victory', was apparently due to the fact that insufficient of the first type had been minted and, in addition, the Governor-General of India was dissatisfied with the rather crude design. Accordingly, a second medal was designed by W. Wyon and struck at the Royal Mint. The obverse carries the diademed head of Queen Victoria with the legend VICTORIA VINDEX (a few medals were struck with the legend VICTORIA REGINA). The reverse shows the winged figure of Victory with wreaths in her right hand and the staff of a Union Jack in her left hand whilst flying over the fortress of Jellala-

bad. Following the curve of the upper half circle of the medal is the inscription JELLALABAD VII APRIL and below in the exergue is the date MDCCCXLII. The recipient's name and regiment are indented on the edge in block capitals. The ribbon, common to both types, is rainbow-pattern watered red, yellow, white and blue, 1.75in wide. The Flying Victories were issued in March 1845 and could be exchanged for the earlier issue; few, however, appear to have availed themselves of the offer.

8.   Defence of Kelat-I-Ghilzie February—May 1842

Kelat-i-Ghilzie was a fort between Cabul and Candahar, garrisoned by some 900 men, mostly Indians, who were besieged for four months. On the obverse of the medal a laurel wreath surmounted by a mural crown, encloses an ornamental shield which bears the name KELAT I GHILZIE in three lines. The reverse shows a trophy of arms which includes a cuirass, surmounted by a caribinier's helmet, above a plaque inscribed INVICTA MDCCCXLII. The general appearance is Victoriana run amok. The ribbon, 1.75in wide, is rainbow-pattern watered red, white, yellow, white and blue and passes through a straight suspender pinned to an ugly clip sweated to the top of the medal. The recipient's name and regiment are engraved in script on the edge. This is a rare medal when named to a verified recipient. There are a number of unnamed and specimen medals on the market.

valued at £3,000,000 were destroyed, and the irate owners refused compensation. In the war that followed, the traditional Chinese fire-breathing dragon heads mounted on the prows of their war junks to terrorise the enemy failed to have the desired effect, and papier mâché dragons came a poor second to British broadsides. The China coastline was completely blockaded and at one point the Emperor of China offered a bounty of 40,000 Chinese dollars for every Englishman, dead or alive. Both the British Commissioner and the Commodore of the British fleet carried a bonus of an extra 10,000 dollars! Amongst the spoils at the end of the war was the island of Hong Kong, ceded in perpetuity, and five trading bases, of which the principal two were Canton and Shanghai.

William Wyon's original, uninhibited design for the campaign medal consisted of a Chinese dragon being savaged by a British lion. More sensitive feelings prevailed, however, and the final reverse shows the arms of England superimposed on a trophy of arms against a palm tree. Above is the inscription ARMIS EXPOSCERE PACEM and in the exergue the word CHINA with the date 1842 underneath. The obverse carries the diademed head of Queen Victoria with the legend VICTORIA REGINA. The medal is worn by a wide (1.5in) crimson ribbon with yellow edges from a straight German silver suspender sweated directly onto the medal. The naming is in bold capitals and the blank spaces filled with stars, similar to the Waterloo medal.

9.　First China War 5th July 1840–29th August 1842

The 'Opium War' as it is popularly known, has a fine, dramatic ring, and conjures up visions of Great Britain trying to stop the rascally heathens from slowly killing themselves with drugs. Unfortunately, the reverse is true and in 1839 it was the Chinese Government which outlawed the importation of opium into their Empire. By way of underlining the edict storage warehouses full of opium, subsequently

10. Scinde Campaign Medals
6th January—24th March 1843

This campaign against the Amirs of Scinde was a direct result of the preceding Afghan War. On 17th February, Major General Sir Charles Napier commanding 2,800 men and 12 guns attacked, and in three hours defeated, 30,000 Scindian infantry supported by 5,000 cavalry and 15 guns. A month later Sir Charles Napier with 5,000 troops attacked and routed the remainder of the enemy, estimated at 20,000 strong, who were entrenched at Duppa, near Hyderabad. The result was the annexation of Scinde and, what was undoubtedly more important to the troops, substantial prize money as the result of vast booty found in the Amirs' palaces. Sir Charles Napier's share amounted to £68,000. The only British regiment present at both engagements was the 22nd Foot (Cheshires) who lost over 200 men killed and wounded.

In common with some of the earlier Indian Campaign awards there are three different strikings of this silver medal, but only the reverses differ. The obverse in each case shows the diademed head of Queen Victoria and the legend VICTORIA REGINA. The lettering on the reverse, in every instance, is surmounted by a crown and surrounded by a wreath.
1. The name MEEANEE above the date 1842.
2. HYDERABAD above the date 1842.
3. MEEANEE HYDERABAD and the date 1843 in three lines, in that order.
The ribbon is 1.75in wide, rainbow-pattern watered red, white, yellow, white and blue and suspended from a large ring or a straight suspender pinned through a steel clip sweated to the medal. The naming is in block capitals or script, but occasionally medals are found unnamed.

11. Gwalior Campaign Stars
December 1843

These stars commemorate two battles fought on the same day, in one of the shortest campaigns ever recorded, against the Mahratta state of Gwalior. The major engagement centred around the village of Maharajpoor where some 18,000 Mahrattas were strongly entrenched with 100 guns. The British army under Sir Hugh Gough was slightly inferior in numbers and decidedly so in artillery, having about 40 guns. The enemy were finally driven from their position after severe hand-to-hand fighting, despite the gallantry of the Gwalior artillerymen who in many cases were bayoneted as they continued to serve the guns. British casualities were about 800 killed and wounded. On the same afternoon, the left wing of the army attacked and routed a small division of the enemy from their position in the hills near Punniar.

The award is a bronze six-pointed star, 1.7in wide and 2in high, made from captured cannon, with a smaller silver centrepiece of similar pattern. In the centre of the small star is the date 29TH

DECR in two lines and in a circle around the date is the name of the action, either PUNNIAR or MAHARAJPOOR and the year 1843. When first issued these stars were fitted with brass hooks and the apparent intention was that they should be worn on the breast of the jacket. Subsequently, many recipients appear to have fitted their own type of suspension, either a straight suspender pinned to the top point of the star or a large ring. Presumably at the same time and quite unofficially, the habit arose of also wearing the star from a ribbon, similar to the Scinde ribbon. The reverse of the star is blank and used for the name and regiment of the recipient, usually in script.

12. Sutlej Campaign Medal 18th December 1845–22nd February 1846. The Sikh Wars

In December 1845 one of the most formidable native powers in India, the Sikh army, trained and in many cases officered by Europeans and supported by excellent artillery, invaded British India. General Gough's army, after a forced march of 150 miles, encountered the Sikh forces, which outnumbered the British by five-to-one, at Moodkee. After heavy fighting and severe losses on both sides, the Sikh army withdrew leaving seventeen guns in British hands. Three days later, on 21st December, reinforced by two battalions of British troops, General Gough moved forward to attack the main Sikh position at Ferozeshuhur. Again the Sikhs resisted ferociously and in the two days' battle that followed the British forces lost one in six of their fighting strength before the enemy was finally defeated. A month later, another Sikh army, having crossed the border, was brought to bay at the village of Aliwal. The British force, outnumbered by two-to-one, was commanded by Sir Harry Smith, later to wear twelve clasps on his Military General Service Medal. The engagement lasted three hours before the Sikhs were routed leaving all their artillery on the field. The 16th Lancers particularly distinguished themselves by charging and breaking an enemy square (losing over 100 men in the process).

The last action of this campaign was fought on the 10th February 1846 at Sobraon where the Sikhs held two miles of entrenchments with 34,000 men, supported by 70 guns and 20,000 reserves. Only about two-fifths of Sir Hugh Gough's army were Europeans, the remainder being native troops. Once again the Sikh army fled in disorder, struggling to escape over the only bridge which spanned the Sutlej river. Finally, the parapet of the bridge collapsed under the press of fugitives and thousands were drowned.

The obverse of the silver medal for this campaign is similar to that of the First China War. The reverse shows the standing figure of Victory with a wreath in her right hand and an olive branch in her left. At her feet is a pile of captured trophies and around the circumference is the legend ARMY OF THE SUTLEJ.

Because the first action in which the recipient fought is given in the exergue, there are four different exergues containing either (1) MOODKEE 1845; (2) FEROZESHUHUR 1845; (3) ALIWAL 1846; or (4) SOBRAON 1846. Three bars were issued, each bearing the name of one of the last three battles. Thus a man who had been in every action received a medal with the exergue MOODKEE 1845, plus three bars. Conversely, a recipient who had been engaged in only the last encounter received a medal with the exergue SOBRAON 1846, without bars. The suspension is an ornamental swivelling suspender and the ribbon dark blue with crimson edges. Naming is impressed in capital letters or Roman skeleton lettering.

AFRICA and in the exergue the date 1853. The ribbon is watered orange with two wide and two narrow dark blue stripes. The obverse was designed by W. Wyon and the reverse by L.C. Wyon. The naming is indented in Roman capitals.

14. Punjab Campaign Medal 7th September 1848– 14th March 1849

This campaign was virtually a continuation of the Sutlej War which had left the militant Sikhs in a state of unrest. The Punjab flared into rebellion in 1848 and the British fielded two armies; one 28,000 strong under Major General Whish besieged the rebel stronghold of Mooltan whilst the second, under Lord Gough, turned northwards towards the Punjab. On 13th January Gough reached Chilianwala where a Sikh army under Sher Singh was entrenched. In the savage battle that followed, where both sides slaughtered the enemy wounded, the British lost several colours, four guns and over 15 per cent of their effective strength. Heaviest casualties were suffered by the South Wales

13. South African Campaigns 1834–1853

This medal was sanctioned on 22nd November 1854 for survivors of the three campaigns against the Kaffirs in South Africa during the years 1834-1835, 1846-1847 and 1850-1853. As this award is dated 1853 it must have been just as confusing for the recipients who earned it in 1843 as it is for collectors today. The only way of determining the campaign for which the medal was awarded is to check the recipient against the regimental roll. Even this is not possible with medals issued to the Naval Brigade which often only show the name and rank. An interesting point connected with these wars is that the wife of Sir Harry Smith (veteran of the Peninsular, India, and Governor of the Colony) was to give her name to a town made famous during the South African War–Ladysmith. Another famous incident connected with the later campaign was the sinking of the troopship *'Birkenhead'* with the officers and men drawn up in parade order on the deck, after the women, children and sick had been safely placed in the boats. Their heroism so impressed King William of Prussia that he ordered an account of the disaster to be read to every unit in the German Army.

The obverse of the medal and suspender is similar to the Punjab award (Medal No. 14), whilst the reverse shows a lion, stopping to drink in front of a bush. Above him are the words SOUTH

28

Borderers who lost 21 officers and 503 other ranks killed or wounded. Both sides withdrew to their respective camps where they were bogged down by three days of torrential rain. However, on 22nd January, Mooltan had been stormed and Whish's troops moved northward to support Gough. Sher Singh struck his camp and moved eastward making for Lahore but on 20th February the combined British forces, totalling 24,000 men and 96 guns caught up with the Sikhs at Goojerat. The battle started at 7am and by early afternoon the enemy were in full retreat, abandoning their guns, wounded and baggage.

A General Order dated 2nd April 1849 granted a medal to all forces employed in the Punjab during the campaign. The reverse of this medal is extremely detailed and shows the Sikh army surrendering their arms and colours in front of a mounted officer. Two regiments of East India troops, complete with colours, are drawn up in the middle distance, whilst in the background there are large palm trees on a hill. Around the top is the legend TO THE ARMY OF THE PUNJAB, and in the exergue the date in Roman numerals MDCCCXLIX. The obverse carries the diademed head of Queen Victoria and the ribbon is dark blue with a yellow stripe on each side, threaded through an ornamental swivelling suspender. Three clasps were issued for the main actions—MOOLTAN, for those engaged in the siege from 7th September 1848 until 22nd January 1849 and CHILIANWALA and GOOJERAT for the two main battles. The maximum number of clasps to any one man was two, although there are numerous medals without clasps awarded to troops who did not participate in any of the three main actions. Naming is in impressed Roman capitals.

15. India General Service Medal 1854–1895

The obverse of this medal and the suspender is similar to those on the Punjab medal. The reverse shows the winged figure of Victory crowning a seated warrior. A lotus flower and four leaves appear in the exergue. The junctions of the suspender, clasp and all the bars are each covered by a rosette, and there are three equal crimson and blue stripes on the ribbon. Twenty-three bars were issued covering a period of forty-one years as follows:

PEGU 28th March 1852-30th June 1853. The second campaign in Burma.

PERSIA 5th December 1856-8th February 1857. A combined naval and army expedition.

NORTH WEST FRONTIER 3rd December 1849-22nd October 1868. Fifteen different campaigns and expeditions spread over nineteen years.

UMBEYLA 20th October-23rd December 1863. An expeditionary force in Hindustan.

BHOOTAN December 1864-February 1866. A four-column punitive force.

LOOSHAI 9th December 1871-20th February 1872. An expedition to recover an abducted planter and his daughter. No British troops were involved.

PERAK 2nd November 1875-20th March 1876. An expedition to Perak which included a naval brigade.

JOWAKI 1877-8 9th November 1877-19th January 1878. The Afridi tribesmen near the Kohat Pass objected to a new road running through their territory.

NAGA 1879-80 December 1879-January 1880. A punitive expedition against the Nagas.

BURMA 1885-7 14th November 1885-30th April 1887. The annexation of Burma.

SIKKIM 1888 15th March-27th
September 1888. A three-cornered
fight with Sikkim which also
involved the Tibetans.
HAZARA 1888. This is generally known
as the Black Mountain Expedition.
BURMA 1887-89 1st May 1887-31st
March 1889. Chiefly this involved
the suppression of quite large scale
banditry, a left-over from the
earlier Burma campaign.
CHIN LUSHAI 1889-90 15th November
1889-30th April 1890. This was
earned by two columns, the Burma
column operating against the Chins
and the Chittagong column in
action with the Lushais.
SAMANA 1891 5th April-25th May 1891.
This was awarded for operations in
the Miranzai Valley and the Samana
Heights.
HAZARA 1891 12th March-16th May
1891. This was for the Hazara Field
Force in the Black Mountains.
N.E. FRONTIER 1891 28th March-7th
May 1891. This clasp was earned
by the Manipur Field Force dealing
with the obstreperous Rajah of
Manipur, a small state adjoining
Assam and Burma.
HUNZA 1891 1st-22 December 1891. A
small but hard-fought campaign
which resulted in three Victoria
Crosses.
BURMA 1889-92 This was for eleven
punitive expeditions, some only
lasting a few days.
LUSHAI 1889-92 11th January 1889-8th
June 1892. This was awarded for
small expeditions into the Lushai
Hills.
CHIN HILLS 1892-93 19th October
1892-10th March 1893. A small
punitive expedition against the
Chins.
KACHIN HILLS 1892-93 3rd December
1892-3rd March 1893. This was for
punitive expeditions into the
Kachin Hills.
WAZIRISTAN 1894-95 22nd October
1894-13th March 1895. A fairly
large expedition against the Wazirs
and a portent of several more
against the same tribes.

A wide variety of naming. Medals with
the last twelve bars were issued in bronze
to native noncombatants.

16.   Crimean War Medal
28th March 1854—
30th March 1856

A monkish squabble over the custody of
keys to a church in the Holy Land was the
ostensible cause which led to the death of
many thousands of men and living misery
for the remainder, who soldiered in
conditions unequalled until the bloody
quagmires of World War I. The official
declaration of war was made on 28th
March 1854 and in the summer the British
and French forces reached Varna in
Bulgaria. The Russians promptly withdrew
and the allies were left with a problem of
finding the enemy. Consequently, in
September the Allied Army sailed for the
Crimea with a loose directive to take
Sebastopol, the Russian base. On 20th
September 1854 the Russians, entrenched
on the heights above the Alma river, were
attacked and defeated. In the war that
followed fleas, flies and fever, coupled
with sunstroke in summer and frostbite in
winter, killed more British troops than the
entire Russian army. Of the 20,425 other
ranks fatalities only 1,933 died of wounds

and 2,598 were killed in action; the remaining 15,894 died of disease. The remaining battles are well known – Balaklava on 25th October 1854; the magnificent charge of Scarlett's Heavy Brigade and the equally magnificent, but useless, charge of the Light Brigade; Inkermann, the 'Soldier's Battle' fought in fog and mist against overwhelming odds on 5th November 1854; and finally, the long weary siege of Sebastopol, culminating in its capture on 9th September 1855. Hostilities were then virtually suspended until peace was signed on 29th March 1856. The futile war was over.

In December 1854 whilst the war was still in progress, the Queen commanded that a medal be awarded to all ranks engaged in the Crimea, with the addition of clasps for Alma or Inkermann for troops engaged at those battles. A clasp was granted for Balaklava in February 1855 and in the following October a further clasp for Sebastopol. Naval forces who operated in the Sea of Azoff were granted a clasp bearing the word AZOFF. The reverse of the medal depicts the winged figure of Victory crowning a Roman warrior with a laurel wreath; the word CRIMEA is inscribed to the left of the figures. On the obverse is the diademed head of Queen Victoria with the legend VICTORIA REGINA round the sides and the date 1854 underneath. The clasps are in the shape of oak leaves, with acorn ornaments, attached to a foliated suspender peculiar to this medal; the ribbon is light blue with yellow edges. Medals were originally issued unnamed but could be returned for naming free of charge in indented capitals. Although a total of five clasps was issued not more than four will be found on any one medal. Medals will be seen bearing single clasps for ALMA, AZOFF or SEBASTOPOL, but anyone entitled to either BALAKLAVA or INKERMANN automatically qualified for SEBASTOPOL. This included members of the Naval Brigade serving ashore. Medals with four clasps to cavalrymen who charged with the Light Brigade are highly prized (and priced) and so, to a lesser extent, are similar medals to the Heavy Brigade.

17. Baltic Medal March 1854–August 1855

After a Fleet Review at Spithead on 23rd April 1856 the Queen commanded that a medal should be awarded to the officers and men of the Royal Navy who had served in the Baltic from March 1854 until the blockade was lifted in 1855. The obverse of the medal is similar to that of the Crimea, except that the date is omitted. On the reverse is a seated figure of Britannia holding a trident and looking over her left shoulder. Behind her are the Russian fortresses of Bormarsund and Sveaborg, while in the foreground is a naval cannon with a pyramid of shot. The word BALTIC is shown around the top and the dates 1854-1855 appear in the exergue. No clasps were awarded, and the ribbon is yellow with blue edges. Apart from about 100 medals awarded to the Royal Sappers and Miners who served on ships, the medal was issued unnamed and is not highly valued. Many recipients, however, had their medals engraved at their own expense, usually including the name of the ship on which they served.

18. India Mutiny Medal 1857–1858

It is well known that greased cartridges started the Indian Mutiny, but like all well known fairy stories it is not quite true. Whilst the Enfield cartridge may have provided the flashpoint, India was already ripe for an explosion in the spring of 1857. The first outbreak occurred at Merrut on Sunday 10th May 1857 and spread throughout Bengal with the holy men prophesying a return of the Mogul dynasty. No doubt readers will be familiar with the main outlines of the rebellion, and the retribution that followed, but two episodes will always be remembered. One was the deliberate action of Conductor Scully, who blew himself and 1,000 mutineers to eternity when he fired the main powder magazine at Delhi; the other is the 'massacre of the innocents' at Cawnpore and the aftermath—one of the few recorded occasions when British troops refused to give quarter. The five main actions for which clasps were subsequently awarded are as follows:

DELHI 30th May-14th September 1857. To troops employed in the re-capture of that city.
DEFENCE OF LUCKNOW 29th June-22nd November 1857. To the original defenders, including about 160 co-opted or volunteer civilians, and also to the first relief force under Havelock.
RELIEF OF LUCKNOW November 1857. To Sir Colin Campbell's force engaged in the relief of the city; these included a British Naval Brigade.
LUCKNOW November 1857-March 1858. Awarded to all forces engaged in the capture of Lucknow.
CENTRAL INDIA January-June 1858. Covered numerous battles and engagements involving the Rajpatana Field Force and the Madras Column. Also for operations in and around Jhansi, Calpee and Gwalior.

In 1858 the Indian Government granted a medal to all armed forces of the Crown and the Honourable East India Company. Two years later the award was extended to all who had borne arms in the suppression of mutiny, including civilians. The obverse of the medal is similar to that Baltic medal. The reverse shows the standing, helmeted figure of Britannia holding a laurel wreath in her outstretched right hand. Over her left arm is the Union Shield and her left hand holds other wreaths (apparently for distribution to the victorious troops). Behind her is a standing British lion and the word INDIA above.

The dates 1857-1858 appear in the exergue. An unusual and ornamental suspender carries the ribbon which has alternate white and red stripes (three of white and two red). The colours are popularly believed to be red for blood and white symbolising the massacred innocents. The recipient's name and unit, or ship, is impressed on the edge in Roman capitals. Although five bars were authorised, the maximum to any one man was four and these only to certain cavalry regiments. Infantry, including the Naval Brigade, could not earn more than two and many medals were issued without clasps. Unlike many mid-Victorian campaign medals, the Indian Mutiny medal was only awarded for service under fire.

19.   Second China War Medal 1857−1860

As far as military historians are concerned the events in China during 1857-8 rank as the second China War. whilst the campaign in 1860 is known as the third China War. However, medal collectors invariably refer to the whole as the second China War because one award covered the three years. (In case this sounds rather complicated, a contemporary account quotes a corporal of the Buffs as referring 'to another do with them bloody yellow "eathen",' so presumably there have always been different points of view among nomenclators). The first fighting was between naval forces but in 1860 the British and French landed forces which began to fight their way overland towards the Taku Forts. During this advance a private soldier of the Buffs, No. 2051 John Moyse, who was in charge of sixteen coolies carrying the rum ration for the force, was captured by Tartar cavalry. The incident that followed, when Moyse refused to kowtow to a mandarin and was beheaded in consequence, made the front page of 'The Times', earned his name a place in the Buffs Regimental Museum and immortalized him in the famous poem by Sir Francis Doyle.

The Taku Forts were successfully stormed on the 21st August 1860 during which the attackers won seven V.C.s. The Chinese, especially their artillerymen, appear to have fought very well, despite stories in English newspapers that they were tied to their guns to prevent them escaping. (Similar tales made the rounds in 1918 about German heavy machine-gun crews). The expeditionary force fought two more quite severe actions before taking Pekin on 13th October 1860. A well directed campaign was somewhat marred by the loss of the Summer Palace in Pekin which the French looted and the British then burned to the ground.

A General Order dated 6th March 1861 awarded a medal to all services engaged in the operations. The obverse is similar to the Indian Mutiny medal whilst the reverse shows the Royal Arms superimposed against a trophy of arms (which appears to include chain shot) in front of a palm tree. Above is the inscription ARMIS EXPOSCERE PACEM and the word CHINA in the exergue. A horn-shaped suspender carries the ribbon which was originally multicoloured with five equally spaced stripes of blue, yellow, red, white and green. A number of medals were certainly issued with this ribbon, but it was later changed to one of crimson with yellow edges. Awards to the Royal Navy were not named, but those to soldiers and marines are named in indented Roman capitals. Six clasps were authorised, the first of which, CHINA 1842 is something of a mystery as a medal had already been awarded for that campaign. Of the remaining five, FATSHAN 1857 and TAKU FORTS 1858 could only be earned by Naval personnel, including marines. The other three clasps were CANTON 1857, TAKU FORTS 1860 and PEKIN 1860. The greatest number of clasps to any one man was five, on a medal to Thomas Cole of the Royal Marine Artillery.

20. New Zealand Medal 1845–1847 and 1860–1866

This award was sanctioned on 1st March 1869, for issue to survivors of those engaged in suppressing the Maori risings in North Island between 1845 and 1846, those in the South Island during 1847 and service generally in New Zealand between 1860 and 1866. It is impossible to itemise the various encounters and engagements; suffice it to say that the Maori proved a worthy and gallant foe and one whose fortified stockades were impregnable to everything except artillery fire. No less than twenty-nine different reverses were struck for this medal, twenty-eight of them bearing different dates, and one undated.

The obverse of the medal shows the head of Queen Victoria, wearing a coronet which holds a veil covering the back of her neck. Around the head is the legend VICTORIA D : G : BRITT : REG : F : D :. On the reverse is a small laurel wreath

which surrounds the date or dates of service. Above are the words NEW ZEALAND and below VIRTUTIS HONOR. Any one of the following dates is shown: 1845-46; 1845-47; 1846-47; 1846; 1847; 1848; 1860; 1860-61; 1860-63; 1860-64; 1860-65; 1860-66; 1861; 1861-63; 1861-64; 1861-65; 1861-66; 1862-66; 1863; 1863-64; 1863-65; 1863-66; 1864; 1864-65; 1864-66; 1865; 1865-66; and 1866. A straight ornamental swivelling suspender, supposed to be fashioned after a fern frond, carried the dark blue ribbon with ⅜in wide red centre stipe. This is a difficult medal to verify as it was not awarded for any particular engagement, but for service in an area during a period of time. In particular, no official actions are recorded between 6th November 1861 and 4th May 1863 but medals were issued bearing, or including, these dates.

21. Canada General Service Medal 1866–1870

Thirty-three years after the first raid, an Army Order of January 1899 authorised the Canadian Government to issue a medal to members of the Imperial forces and Canadian Militia who had been engaged in the Fenian Raids and the Red River Expedition under Colonel Wolseley. At the end of the American Civil War the Fenians (sworn to liberate Ireland from the yoke of England) decided to start their programme by liberating Canada. The invading army, numbers uncertain, under O'Neill, proved no match for the Canadian Militia and were hustled back over the U.S. border, where many of them were arrested. The second raid coincided with a rebellion led by self-styled 'General' Louis Reil, whose supporters occupied Fort Garry, imprisoned many residents and seized the Hudson Bay Company's treasury. The second Fenian raid promptly dispersed when confronted by the Canadian Militia and the rebellion collapsed on the arrival of Imperial and Canadian forces. Reil escaped however, and was responsible for a second rebellion fifteen years later.

On the obverse of the medal is a veiled bust of Queen Victoria with the legend VICTORIA REGINA ET IMPERATRIX. The reverse shows the Canadian flag surrounded by a maple wreath and above it the word CANADA. The ribbon has equal vertical divisions of red, white and red. Three bars were issued–FENIAN RAID 1866; FENIAN RAID 1870 and RED RIVER 1870 and the medal was never awarded without a bar or bars. Just over 16,000 medals were issued, but only 20 of these carried all three bars. Naming is usually impressed in square capitals.

22.   Abyssinian War Medal 4th October 1867–19th April 1868

Theodore, King of Abyssinia, having imprisoned and held in chains a number of British and German subjects, including the British Consul, it became necessary to point out the error of his ways. The expeditionary force under Sir Robert Napier was extremely well organized, particularly regarding transport and medical facilities, and the camp followers and drivers far exceeded in numbers the 14,000 troops, including a naval brigade. This is a disappointing award for those who like 'blood' on their medals as the total British casualties amounted to 66, of whom 29 were wounded and the remaining 37 died of disease.

The medal, authorised by a General Order dated 1st March 1869, is very distinctive and much smaller than usual (1.25in diameter). The obverse shows a coroneted and veiled bust of Queen Victoria within a beaded circle and surrounded by a nine-pointed star. Between each angle of the points is one of the letters of the word ABYSSINIA.

On the reverse, in a beaded circle surrounded by a wreath of laurel, is embossed the recipient's name, rank and unit or ship. The medal is suspended from a silver swivel ring attached to a crown soldered to the top of the piece. The ribbon is 1.5in wide, white, with a broad red stripe down the centre. It should be noted that some of the awards to Indian troops had the recipient's details engraved. This is probably one of the most expensive campaign medals ever struck as the embossing necessitated a separate die for each award.

23. Ashantee War Medal
9th June 1873–4th February 1874

This medal, authorised on 1st June 1874,
was awarded for Sir Garnet Wolseley's
campaign against the Ashanti in the Gold
Coast, or Ghana as it is now known. Again
the casualties were very light and disease
incapacitated far more troops than the
enemy. This was the only occasion when
the Martini-Henry Elcho bayonet was used
on active service. A 20in blade swelling to
a double-edged spear point with saw
serrations on the back edge, this was
supposed to serve a double purpose in
both killing the enemy and clearing a
passage through the undergrowth.

On the obverse of the piece is the
legend VICTORIA REGINA above the
diademed head of Queen Victoria, wearing
a veil. The reverse is filled to capacity with
bodies and branches, allegedly British
troops fighting natives in the bush. The
ribbon is 1.25in wide, yellow with black
borders and two thin black stripes down
the centre. The naming is in indented
capitals and the date 1873-4 is also shown.
One bar COOMASSIE was awarded to all
those who crossed the River Prah and also
troops engaged in either of the actions at
Amoaful and Ardahsa on 31st January and
4th February 1874 respectively.

24. Zulu and Basuto War Medal
25th September 1877−2nd December 1879

This medal was sanctioned in 1880 and is similar to that for the previous South African campaigns between 1834 and 1853 except for the substitution of a Zulu shield and four crossed assegais for the date in the exergue. The name of the recipient and his unit is engraved on the rim in capital letters. Although it was possible to earn the medal without a bar (for service in Natal between 11th January

and 1st September 1879) it was usually issued with one of five dated bars—1877-8 for actions against the Galekas; 1878 for operations involving the Griquas; 1879 the Zulu War or the mopping up operations against Chiefs Sekukini or Moirosi and 1878-9 or 1877-8-9 for men engaged in more than one campaign.

Medals to men who fought in the main actions of the Zulu War (Isandhlwana, Rorke's Drift and Ulundi) usually command a much higher price than awards for the other campaigns. The invasion of Zululand began on 11th January 1879 and despite the fact that the Zulus, under Cetewayo, were one of the most powerful military nations Africa had ever seen (they had defeated the Boers on more than one occasion) the British commander, Lord Chelmsford, seems to have grossly under-estimated his enemy.

One of the invading columns halted at Isandhlwana, some miles inside Zululand, but no attempt was made to fortify the temporary camp. On 22nd January 1879 it was attacked by a Zulu army of about 14,000 men led by Dambulamanzi, Cetewayo's half-brother, and the invaders massacred almost to a man. Elated by their success, part of the Zulu army moved down the Tugela river where, on the Natal side, stood two stone buildings with thatched roofs. Originally a Swedish mission station and now doing duty as a military hospital and store depot, the name of the post was to become part of British military history—Rorke's Drift. The small garrison began building a parapet of biscuit boxes but this was only two boxes high when the first Zulu attack was launched at 4-30pm. Time and time again throughout the night waves of Zulu warriors attempted to storm the post. Finally, at dawn the next morning, the enemy withdrew leaving over 400 of their dead on or around the post. The garrison had lost 17 men killed and 5 of their sick men burned to death when the hospital was fired. They had also won eight Victoria Crosses, including one to Corporal Scheiss of the Natal Native Contingent, originally a patient in the hospital and the only Swiss national ever to gain this award. News of Isandhlwana meanwhile created a sensation in England and strong reinforcements were hurried out to the Cape. However, even before they reached the front the Zulus suffered a crushing defeat at Ulundi. Cetewayo's retreat was turned into a rout by three squadrons of the 17th Lancers, supported by mounted infantry and volunteers, who pursued the beaten army for seven miles.

25. Afghanistan 1878–1880

The causes of the second Afghan war in the 'training ground' of the British Army are too many to enumerate here; suffice it to say that Afghanistan was invaded by three British columns who fought a series of actions. In one of these, at the battle of Maiwand on 27th July 1880, a British and Indian force was overwhelmed by Afghans and the survivors besieged in Kandahar. This defeat was lightened by the gallantry of the 66th Foot (Royal Berkshires) who covered the retreat of the remainder of the column until only eleven men were left on their feet. Surrounded by 10,000 Afghans and Ghazis and accompanied only by their regimental mascot, a small white dog, these eleven Berkshire men, who had fired all their ammunition, refused to surrender. Instead they charged! Needless to say, the battle of Maiwand (nearly a thousand casualties, most of them killed) did not merit a bar, but the action at Ali Masjid (fourteen killed) earned a clasp and battle honours.

On 19th March 1881 a medal was granted which showed on the obverse the crowned draped bust of Queen Victoria and the legend VICTORIA REGINA ET IMPERATRIX. The reverse is crowded with elephant-borne artillery, mounted and foot soldiers with a fortress-capped mountain in the background. In the top left hand arc is the word AFGHANISTAN and the dates 1878-79-80 in the exergue. The ribbon is green with crimson stripes on each edge. Six bars were authorised but not more than four could be earned by any one man. ALI MUSJID 21st November 1878; PEIWAR KOTAL 2nd December.1878; CHARASIA 6th October 1879; KABUL 10-23 December 1879; AHMED KHEL 19th April 1880 and KANDAHAR 1st September 1880. Medals to British troops were engraved in squat or sloping capitals whilst those issued to natives were named in capitals or sloping script.

26. Kabul to Kandahar Star 9th–31st August 1880

This bronze star, made from captured cannon taken at the battle of Kandahar, was awarded to all who had taken part in General Robert's famous march to relieve Kandahar. It is a five-pointed star with a ball between the inner angles, except the top one. In the centre is the monogram VR1 around which is a circular raised border. In raised lettering on this border are the words KABUL TO KANDAHAR with the date 1880 at the bottom. The reverse is plain with a hollow centre. The star is surmounted by a crown to which is attached a ring, 7/10ths in diameter, which holds the typical India pattern rainbow red, white, yellow, white and blue ribbon. There is engraved naming on the reverse, capital letters for British troops and capitals or sloping script for Indian soldiers.

27. Cape of Good Hope General Service Medal 1880–1897

This medal was issued in 1900 by the Cape Government, with the approval of the Crown, to Colonial troops and a small number of British officers and men who had been engaged in suppressing small risings in the places named on the bars.

The obverse shows the crowned bust of Queen Victoria and the legend VICTORIA REGINA ET IMPERATRIX. On the reverse is the arms of Cape Colony with the motto SPES BONA. The ribbon has equal vertical bands of dark blue, light biscuit and dark blue. The three bars are TRANSKEI 13th September 1880-13th May 1881 for operations in Tembuland and Griqualand East, where the natives refused to hand in their firearms; BASUTOLAND 13th September 1880-27th April 1881 sporadic fighting as a result of which Basutoland became a Crown Colony in March 1884; and BECHUANALAND 24th December 1896-30th July 1897, where a native revolt was suppressed.

28. Egypt 1882–1889

Mehemit Ali, Khedive of Egypt, notorious for his women, gambling and what the literature of the period guardedly calls 'unnatural appetites' was obliged to sell his Suez Canal shares to Great Britain. Shortly afterwards he was replaced by his son Tewfik who had inherited all his father's vices and invented some of his own. The state of the country worsened and in 1882 the army, which had not been paid or clothed for several years, mutinied under Arabi Pasha. Arabi threatened to seize the Suez Canal (all this has a familiar ring) and began to strengthen the forts guarding Alexandria. On 11th July 1882 after an ultimatum the British fleet bombarded the fortifications and landed seamen and marines to restore order.

Britain was now committed to restore law and order, and an attack was made on the rebel army who had entrenched themselves at Tel-el-Kebir. Guided by naval officers with compasses the British force made a night march across the desert and routed the enemy. An occupational force of 10,000 men was left in Egypt, and a General Order of 1882 granted a medal with appropriate bars to those engaged in the two battles.

Britain now found herself responsible for a country without revenue, an army or administration. At this awkward moment in time there appeared in the Sudan, nominally ruled by Egypt, the Mahdi or 'Expected One', a religious fanatic whose puritanical control over his dervishes

Egypt medal and the medal itself was re-issued in 1884 but with a plain exergue.

The obverse of the medal is similar to that for Ashantee, (No. 23). The first reverse shows a simple design of the Sphinx with the word EGYPT above and the date 1882 below. The ribbon has three bright blue and two white stripes of equal width. Dated medals are engraved in sloping capitals, as are the second issue to British troops. Undated medals issued to Indian troops are engraved in small running script and those awarded to the Egyptian army are named in Arabic. The clasps are as follows:

ALEXANDRIA 11th JULY 1882; TEL-EL-KEBIR 13th September 1882; EL-TEB 29th February 1884; TAMAII 13th March 1884; EL-TEB-TAMAII (To those who took part in both actions); SUAKIN 1884; THE NILE 1884-85 (awarded to those who served in the expedition to relieve Gordon); ABU KLEA 17th January 1885. A savage engagement and the only recorded instance when a British square broke; KIRBEKAN (in common with the previous clasp, this bar is always found in conjunction with that for THE NILE 1884-85); SUAKIN 1885; TOFREK (always found in conjunction with the previous bar); GEMAIZAH 20th December 1888; TOSKI 3rd August 1889.

would have made Cromwell green with envy. To suppress the rebellion an Egyptian army of some 10,000 led by Hicks Pasha marched out against the dervishes. Although the force looked impressive on paper, many of the men had been released from prison following their part in the 1882 mutiny and 51 men of the Krupp battery managed to desert en route although chained to their guns. The result was a foregone conclusion and at the beginning of November the army was slaughtered and all their guns and nearly a million rounds of ammunition fell into the hands of the Mahdi. After a series of further engagements the British Government decided to withdraw from the Sudan. 'Chinese' Gordon was appointed to undertake the evacuation of garrisons and civil staff, but by the end of 1884 Gordon was besieged in Khartoum. The relief column fought its way up the Nile, only to arrive forty-eight hours too late to prevent the fall of the city and Gordon's murder. During the course of the next five years, eleven more clasps were authorised for the

THE KHEDIVE'S STARS. Five-pointed bronze stars were awarded by the Khedive to all recipients of the Egypt medal.

29. North West Canada 1885

This medal was sanctioned for issue on 18th September 1885 to all who had taken part in the suppression of Riel's Rebellion. Riel, who had escaped from Fort Garry in 1870, set up a provisional government and promised heaven on earth to his supporters, mainly Fenians and local Indians. Most of the Canadian militia were involved and the rising was speedily suppressed. Riel was unable to try the principle of 'third time lucky' as he was expeditiously tried and hanged.

The obverse of the medal is similar to that awarded for the Ashantee War. The reverse has the words NORTH WEST CANADA surrounded by a maple wreath and the date 1885 in the centre. The ribbon is blue-grey in colour with two red stripes two millimetres from each edge. The medals were issued unnamed, but many are found named in block letters. One bar SASKATCHEWAN was awarded to all those who had fought in any of the three main actions of the rebellion, namely at the Saskatchewan and Fish Rivers and Batoche. No British troops were present except for nine officers on the Canadian Staff.

30. East and West Africa 1887–1900

Whilst this medal is slightly thinner than that issued for the Ashantee campaign of 1873-74, (plate 23), it is otherwise identical, even to the ribbon and suspension. Recipients of the Ashantee medal only gained the appropriate bar for further service in East and West Africa between the dates shown, and not another medal. Twenty-three bars were authorised but for some peculiar reason the M'wele campaign in 1895-96 failed to qualify for a bar; instead the name and date were engraved round the rim. The bars are as follows:

1887-8 13th November 1887-2nd January 1888. For operations against the Tonnie Tribe.

WITU 1890 17th-27th October 1890. A punitive expedition against the Sultan of Witu.

1891-2 29th December 1891-2nd February 1892. An expedition to Gambia.

1892 8th March-25th May 1892. Expeditions against Tambi, Toniataba and the Jebus.

WITU AUGUST 1893 7th-13th August 1893. More trouble with the Sultan of Witu.

LIWONDI 1893 February-March 1893. A small naval force against Chief Liwondi.

JUBA RIVER 1893 23rd-25th August 1893. A small volunteer force against the Somalis.

LAKE NYASSA 1893 November 1893. Another volunteer boat party against a local chief.

1893-94 16th November 1893-11th March 1894. Operations in Sierra Leone and Gambia.

GAMBIA 1894 23rd February-13th March 1894. This commemorates some heavy fighting and casualties for the naval brigade involved.

BENIN RIVER 1894 August-September 1894. An expedition chiefly naval, up the Benin River.

BRASS RIVER 1895 17th-26th February 1895. Operations against King Koko.

1896-98 27th November 1896-27th June 1898. This was awarded for several punitive expeditions into the Northern Territories of the Gold Coast.

NIGER 1897 6th January-26th February. An expedition to Western Provinces.

BENIN 1897 6th February-7th August. A punitive column to Benin territory.

DAWKITA 1897 28th March 1897. The defence of Dawkita against Sofa tribesmen, in the Gold Coast.

1897-98 September 1897-August 1898. Expeditions, chiefly against the Ebos by Lagos Frontier Force.

1898. Conditions similar to the previous bar.

SIERRA LEONE 1898-99 18th February 1898-9th March 1899. Two expeditions involving native troops and a naval brigade.

1899 February-May 1899. Expeditions in Southern Nigeria.

1900 4th January-8th May 1900. An expedition to Kaduna and against the Munshis in the Northern Province.

31. British South Africa Company's Medal 1890–1897

There are four different reverses to this
award, although the obverse is the same in
each case, namely the bust of Queen
Victoria, crowned and veiled, with the
legend VICTORIA REGINA. The reverse
shows a speared charging lion with a native
shield and spears in the foreground.
Below, in two lines, are the words
BRITISH SOUTH AFRICA COMPANY.
Above is the name and date of the
campaign: 1. MATABELELAND 1893;
2. RHODESIA 1896; 3. MASHONALAND
1897 and 4. no place or date, which was
authorised for the Mashonaland campaign
of 1890. The first medal was sanctioned
by Queen Victoria in 1896; the last was
authorised by King George V in 1927—
thirty-seven years after the incident. The
medal is larger than usual and is 1.45in in
diameter. The ribbon is 1.4in wide and
orange-yellow with three narrow blue
stripes, one in the centre and one 3mm
from each edge. The suspender is an
ornate affair, too wide for the ribbon, and
is a mass of roses, shamrocks and thistles.
    Four bars were issued:

MASHONALAND 1890. More in the
        nature of a flag and survey expedi-
        tion.
MATABELELAND 1893. The first
        Matabele War including Major
        Wilson's epic stand with thirty men
        on the Shangani River.
RHODESIA 1896. Small scale revolts by
        the Matabele and Mashona tribes.
MASHONALAND 1897. A fairly large
        rebellion and heavy fighting.

32. Central Africa 1891–1898

This medal is identical on both the obverse
and reverse with the East and West Africa
medal (No. 30) previously described. The
ribbon has vertical equal bands of black,
white and terracotta, suspended by means
of a small swivelling ring affixed to a claw
at the top of the medal. Naming varies.
The medal was first issued to commemorate a number of small campaigns in
Central and East Africa between 1891 and
1894. It was re-issued in 1899 for operations in British Central Africa between
1894 and 1898. On the last occasion it
was fitted with a plain suspender and a bar
CENTRAL AFRICA 1894-98 was added.
Men who had already received the first
issue received only the bar and had the
rings removed from their original medal
and replaced by the straight suspender.

same flag. The word INDIA is on the left and the date 1895 on the right. The ornamental suspender and rosettes are the same type as those fitted to the India General Service 1854 medal and the ribbon has three vertical bands of crimson and two of dark green, interspaced. These awards were generally named in script except for the Highland Light Infantry whose medals were named in block capitals. Seven bars were issued, but as Queen Victoria died before the issue of the seventh, the medal was re-struck. This second issue shows the bust of King Edward VII in Field Marshal's uniform and the legend EDWARVS VII REX IMPERATOR. In all other respects it is the same as the first issue. All these medals were awarded in bronze to native non-combatants.

The bars are as follows:

DEFENCE OF CHITRAL 1895 3rd March-19th April 1895. A seven week siege of a small garrison.

RELIEF OF CHITRAL 1895 7th March-15th August 1895. For the Relief column which fought through to the garrison.

PUNJAB FRONTIER 1897-98 10th June 1897-6th April 1898. For the defenders of Shabkadr Fort, Mohmand Field Force and Tirah Expeditionary Force.

MALAKAND 1897 26th July-2nd August 1897. For the defence and relief of Chakdara and Malakand.

SAMANA 1897 22nd August-2nd Octobei 1897. For operations on Samana Ridge defence of Fort Gulistan and the 21 Sikh defenders of Saragai post who held off 10,000 Afridis for four days before being overrun and massacred.

TIRAH 1897-98 2nd October 1897-6th April 1898. This bar, never issued singly, was awarded to the Tirah Expeditionary Force which included the Kurram and Peshawar Columns and the Rawalpindi Brigade. Troops on lines of communications and the Swat Valley also received this bar, and as the principle Afridi amusement was attacking convoys it was well earned. Unlike the handful of casualties behind many of the campaign bars, Tirah commemorates over 300 killed and nearly a thousand wounded.

WAZIRISTAN 1901-2 23rd November 1901-10th March 1902. The bar was awarded with the second issue medal for four months of roadmaking, fighting and raids against the Mahsuds.

33.   India Medal 1895 − 1902

The obverse of this medal is similar to plate 21 (the Canada General Service award), whilst the reverse shows a British and an Indian soldier both supporting the

34.   Ashanti Star 1896 7th December 1895—17th January 1896

Further trouble on the Gold Coast, including torture, cannibalism, human sacrifices and other unneighbourly behaviour led to the Ashanti Expedition, comprising about 2,000 troops. A distinctive gun metal star was awarded for this campaign consisting of a four-pointed star bisected by a St. Andrew's Cross. In the centre is the Imperial crown surrounded by a raised band inscribed ASHANTI on top and the date 1896 below. On the reverse, in raised lettering, are the words FROM THE QUEEN. The star is suspended by means of a ring attached to the top of the upper point, and the ribbon is yellow with a black stripe 2mm from each edge. It was issued unnamed, but the 2nd Battalion of the West Yorkshire Regiment had their awards named at their Colonel's expense.

35. Queens' Sudan Medal 1896—97

In 1899 this medal was awarded to the armed forces engaged in the reconquest of the Sudan. The obverse is similar to the East and Central Africa medal (plate 37). The reverse, which is particularly well balanced, shows the seated figure of Victory holding a palm branch in her right hand and a laurel wreath in her left, against a background of four British and Egyptian flags. Her feet rest on a plinth bearing the word SUDAN which is supported by three lilies. The ribbon is yellow and black, divided by a thin vertical stripe of red. These colours are supposed to represent the yellow desert and black dervishes and in between the 'thin red line' of British troops. No battle clasps were issued. Naming varies considerably.

36. Khedive's Sudan Medal 1896—1908

Troops engaged in this campaign were also given the Khedive's Sudan Medal which was instituted in 1897 and continued to be awarded until 1908, by which time a total of fifteen bars had been added. It is, however, rarely found with more than two bars (Khartoum and Atbara) to British troops although some Egyptians and Sudanese earned as many as ten clasps. The obverse of the medal carries an Arabic inscription while the reverse shows an oval shield with three stars and crescents thereon, superimposed on a trophy of arms. The whole rests on a plinth inscribed in Arabic THE RECONQUEST OF THE SUDAN 1314 (The Mohammedan year 1314 corresponded with 1897 in the Western calendar). The straight suspender holds the 1.5in wide yellow ribbon with a vertical broad blue stripe down the middle, symbolical of the Nile flowing through the desert.

THE ATBARA was awarded for the battle of that name fought on 8th April 1898 against a Dervish army commanded by Emir Mahmoud. It is usually found in conjunction with KHARTOUM which was in fact awarded for the Battle of

Omdurman and the famous charge of the 21st Lancers on 2nd September, 1898. Although Khartoum was entered after the battle, it is difficult to surmise why a battle clasp should bear any name other than that of the engagement for which it was awarded. No doubt those responsible found ample precedent in that the first two clasps for the 1854 India General Service medal were given for actions outside India (i.e. Burma and Persia) whilst the bar COOMASSIE on the 1873 Ashantee medal commemorates a battle at Amoaful.

The other clasps are as follows:

FIRKET 7th June 1806; HAFIR 19th-26th September 1896; ABU HAMED 7th July 1897; SUDAN 1897 15th July-6th November 1897; GEDAREF 7th September-26th December 1898; GEDID 22nd November 1899; SUDAN 1899; BAHR-EL-GHAZAL 1900-02 13th December 1900-27th April 1902; JEROK January-March 1904; NYAM-NYAM January-May 1905; TALODI 2nd-15th June 1905; KATFIA April 1908; NYIMA 1st-21st November 1908.

37. East and Central Africa 1897–1899

This award superseded the Central Africa
Medal 1891-8. On the obverse is the
half-length figure of Queen Victoria
wearing a small crown and veil and holding
a sceptre in her right hand with the
familiar legend VICTORIA REGINA ET
IMPERATRIX. The obverse shows
Britannia holding a trident in her right
hand and standing in front of a magnificent British Lion. The sun rises in the right
background and in the exergue are the
words EAST & CENTRAL AFRICA. The
ribbon is half yellow and half red. Naming
is in thin sloping or upright capitals. The
medal, without bars, was awarded to
certain native bearers.

The following four bars were
authorised:

LUBWA'S 23rd September 1897-24th
February 1898. For operations
against a battalion of mutinous
Sudanese troops who had to be
driven out of Fort Lubwa.
UGANDA 1897-98 20th July 1897-19th
March 1898. Military operations in
the Protectorate.
1898 21st March-2nd May 1899. Action
against a Somali tribe.
UGANDA 1899 21st March-2nd May
1899. Further operations within
the Protectorate.

38. Queen's South Africa Medal
11th October 1899–31st May 1902

In common with many other wars which 'will be over by Christmas' it appears that the probable duration of a campaign against some rebellious farmers was grossly underestimated, and the first issue of this medal bore the dates 1899-1900 on the reverse. This was speedily rectified but the dates are still visible on many pieces, especially when they are 'toned'.

'He who fights and runs away lives to fight another day' should have been coined about the Boer, even if it wasn't. Hardy, practical and an expert shot, afraid of nothing other than a cavalry lance (which he regarded as a barbaric weapon to use against white men) the Boer saw nothing glorious in war and had no intention of dying, other than from ripe old age. Having picked off two or three of the 'red-necks' who advanced against him in Aldershot parade ground formation, there was no future in remaining to be bayoneted, nor was there any ignominy in retreat. He would mount his pony, laagered never far to the rear, and gallop off the to the next line of defences to repeat the process, or work round the flanks. Backed by well trained artillery and foreign volunteers, the Boers taught the British soldier lessons in tactics, fieldcraft and sniping. Fourteen years later, these lessons learned and assimilated would enable a British Corps to hold back a German Army at Mons, but in 1899 the lessons had still be learned the hard way at a cost of nearly 30,000 casualties.

The obverse of the medal is similar to plate 42 for the Third China War. The reverse shows Britannia with a standard in her left hand holding out a laurel wreath to advancing troops. In the left background are two men-of-war and following the top half circle are the words SOUTH AFRICA. There were two different strikings of this reverse; in the first Britannia's wreath points to the R in Africa whereas in the second it points to the F. These strikings do not affect the price of the medal. A broad orange band constitutes the middle of the ribbon, which is flanked on either side by a blue stripe and a wider red stripe. Naming varies considerably and owing to the staggering number of Imperial, Colonial, volunteer and auxiliary formations engaged, it is often difficult to decipher a unit which is only represented by initials.

C.C.C.C. for example stands for Cape Colony Cyclist Corps and C.M.S.C.-Corps of Military Staff Clerks! Bronze medals without bars were awarded to certain Indian and West Indian troops and native bearers.

Twenty-six bars were issued, of which five are termed 'State' bars, that is they were awarded for various small actions in the various states, two are dated bars and the remainder are battle or engagement clasps. The maximum number of bars to any one medal is nine to the Army and eight to the Navy. Nobody could be awarded both the CAPE COLONY and NATAL bars together, although the medal rolls show that Pte. Wingell, a Royal Marine attached to the army, managed the impossible. The bars are:

CAPE COLONY 11th October 1899-31st May 1902; NATAL 11th October 1899-17th May 1900; RHODESIA 11th October 1899-17th May 1900; RELIEF OF MAFEKING 17th May 1900; DEFENCE OF KIMBERLEY 15th October 1899-15th February 1900; TALANA 20th October 1899; ELANDS-LAAGTE 21st October 1899; DEFENCE OF LADYSMITH 3rd November 1899-28th February 1900; BELMONT 23rd November 1899; MODDER RIVER 28th November 1899; TUGELA HEIGHTS 12th-27th February 1900; RELIEF OF KIMBERLEY 15th February 1900; PAADERBERG 17th-26th February 1900; ORANGE FREE STATE 28th February 1900-31st May 1902; RELIEF OF LADYSMITH 15th December 1899-28th February 1900; DRIEFONTEIN 10th March 1900; WEPENER 9th-25th April 1900; DEFENCE OF MAFEKING 13th October 1899–17th May 1900; TRANSVAAL 24th May 1900–31st May 1902; JOHANNESBURG 31st May 1900; LAING'S NEK 12th June 1901; DIAMOND HILL 11th-12th June 1900; WITTEBERGEN 1st-29th July 1900; BELFAST 26th-27th August 1900; SOUTH AFRICA 1901; SOUTH AFRICA 1902.

These last two bars were awarded to those not eligible for the King's medal although they served at the front during 1901 or from 1st January to 31st May 1902.

39. King's South Africa Medal 1901–1902

As Queen Victoria died during the South Africa War, King Edward VII authorised this medal to be awarded to all those who were serving in South Africa on or after 1st January 1902 and would complete eighteen months service before 1st June 1902. It was always issued in conjunction with the Queen's medal and never issued without a bar, except to nearly 600 nursing sisters.

The obverse of the medal is similar to that on the second striking of the 1895 India General Service medal, while the reverse and mounting are the same as the Queen's South Africa medal. The ribbon, however, is green, white and yellow in equal widths.

40. Queen's Mediterranean Medal 1899–1902

This medal is precisely the same as the Queen's South Africa medal, except that the word MEDITERRANEAN is substituted for SOUTH AFRICA on the reverse. It was awarded to garrisons in the Mediterranean, including St. Helena, an important Boer P.O.W. camp. No bars were awarded.

41. Transport Medal 1899 –1902

The obverse has the bust of King Edward
VII in the uniform of an Admiral of the
Fleet and the legend EDWARDVS VII
REX ET IMPERATOR and the reverse
shows a map of most of the world with a
steamship and below the inscription OB
PATRIAM MILITIBUS PER MARE
TRANSVECTIS ADJUTAM. The ribbon is
red with a blue stripe, 5mm wide inset
3mm from each edge. There are two bars:
SOUTH AFRICA 1899-1902 and CHINA
1900. This medal was sanctioned on 8th
November 1903 for award to senior
officers of troop transports to the South
Africa War and the Boxer Rebellion.

(Both this and the preceding award are
included only for reference; neither, by
any stretch of the imagination, can be
termed campaign medals, as it was not
possible for the recipient to be in action!
Perhaps they are better described as
interesting curios.)

42. Third China War 1900 10th June–31st December 1900

This war is usually known as the Boxer
Rebellion, derived from the members of a
Chinese secret society known as 'Fists of
Righteous Harmony' or 'Boxers'. A wave
of looting and murder, including at least
one missionary burned alive, proved
neither righteous nor harmonious and the
major powers landed an allied expeditionary force to restore order.

Although the medal was not issued
until the reign of Edward VII, it had been
approved by Queen Victoria and bore on
the obverse her crowned and veiled head
with the legend VICTORIA REGINA ET
IMPERATRIX. The reverse was similar to
the China medal of 1860 but the date
1900 was added under CHINA in the
exergue. The ribbon is crimson with full
yellow edges 6mm wide. The naming is
indented in thin block capitals. The locally
recruited coolie corps received unnamed
bronze medals.

The three bars were issued as follows:
TAKU FORTS, DEFENCE OF LEGA-
TIONS and RELIEF OF PEKIN. The
clasps for the legations were issued to 82
British troops, who formed part of the
Legation guard of just over 400, and these
are very rare.

43. Ashanti 31st March–25th December 1900

This medal was sanctioned in October 1901 and granted to men of the Ashanti Field Force who had suppressed a native rising. It was the first medal to be awarded in the reign of Edward VII, and the obverse shows his bust with the legend EDWARDVS VII REX IMPERATOR. The reverse portrays a British Lion standing on a rock with a native shield and two assegais thereon. Beneath, in a small scroll, is the word ASHANTI. The sun rises in the left background. The ribbon is dark green with a black stripe 4½mm wide, on each edge and in the centre. One bar inscribed KUMASSI was awarded to troops who defended, or relieved, the town of that name between 31st March and 15th July 1900. The medal in bronze was given to native bearers.

44. Africa General Service Medal 1902–1956

The obverse of this medal is the same as that of the King's South Africa Medal (plate 39) and the reverse is similar to that for East and Central Africa (plate 37), except that the one word AFRICA appears in the exergue. The ribbon is yellow, edged with black and with two narrow green stripes equidistant in the middle.

Thirty-four bars were issued with this medal; a further ten for the second issue bearing the head of King George V and one for the third issue with the head of Queen Elizabeth II. As we have given away, withdrawn from, or been thrown out of our African possessions it seems unlikely that there will ever be a forty-sixth bar to this medal. It would take far too long even to outline the circumstances leading to the award of all these bars; but the list of names on the clasps is as follows:

N.NIGERIA; N.NIGERIA 1902; N.NIGERIA 1903; N.NIGERIA 1903-4; N.NIGERIA 1904; N.NIGERIA 1906; S.NIGERIA; S.NIGERIA 1902; S.NIGERIA 1902-03; S.NIGERIA 1903; S.NIGERIA 1903-04; S.NIGERIA 1904; S.NIGERIA 1904-5; S.NIGERIA 1905; EAST AFRICA 1902; EAST AFRICA 1904; EAST AFRICA 1905; EAST AFRICA 1906; WEST AFRICA 1906; WEST AFRICA 1908; WEST AFRICA 1909-10; SOMALILAND 1901; SOMALILAND 1902-4; JIDBALLI; SOMALILAND 1908-10; B.C.A. 1899-1900 (British Central Africa); JUBULAND; GAMBIA; ARO 1901-02; LANGO 1901; KISSI 1905; NANDI 1905-06; SHIMBER BERRIS 1914-15; NYASALAND 1915; EAST AFRICA 1913; EAST AFRICA 1914; EAST AFRICA 1913-14; EAST AFRICA 1915; JUBULAND 1917-18; EAST AFRICA 1918; NIGERIA 1918; SOMALILAND 1920 (the first time troops were conveyed by aircraft carrier, H.M.S. Ark Royal) and KENYA 21st October 1952 to 17th November 1956.

45. Tibet Medal 13th December 1903—23rd September 1904

This award was authorised in February 1905 for all members of the Tibet Mission and accompanying troops who served at or beyond Silgari between the dates shown. Very few British troops were present and consquently medals to Europeans are scarce. The obverse carries a bust of Edward VII in Field Marshal's uniform and the legend EDWARDVS VII KAISAR-I-HIND. In shallow relief on the reverse is a representation of the fortress of Lhasa and underneath are the words TIBET 1903-4. The ribbon has a maroon centre flanked by a white stripe on each side and 6mm wide green stripes on each edge. One bar GYANTSE was given to those who defended, or relieved, that fort.

46. Zulu Rebellion 8th February–3rd August 1906

Granted by the Natal Government in 1908 to all those who had taken part in the suppression of the Zulu rising in 1906. On the obverse is the coinage head of King Edward VII and the legend EDWARDVS VII REX IMPERATOR. The reverse is somewhat complicated and has a female figure, representing Natal, holding the sword of Justice in her right hand and a palm branch in her left. She stands on some scattered native weapons and is supported by Britannia. In the background are some natives and a krall, whilst the rising sun shows in the right. The word NATAL appears in the exergue, and the ribbon is crimson with black edges. It was generally issued with a bar with the date 1906 thereon.

47. India General Service Medal 1908–1935

In December 1908 a new Indian General Service medal was issued for the North West Frontier campaign of that year. It was also the last medal struck in the reign of Edward VII. There were three issues of this particular medal, but the reverse was the same in each case and shows Jamrud Fort with Khyber Pass in the background. Below is the word INDIA partly framed by a branch of laurel and another of oak. The ribbon is green with a dark blue stripe 15mm wide in the centre, and hangs from a floral suspender with rosettes, in common with all previous Indian General Service medals. The obverse of the first issue is similar to the Tibet medal. The second issue, which started with the medal given with the bar for ABOR 1911-12, has the crowned bust of King George V in robes and the legend GEORGIVS V KAISAR-I-HIND. The third issue began with the award given with the bar for NORTH WEST FRONTIER 1930-31 and again showed the crowned bust of King George V in robes, but with the legend GEORGIVS.V.D.G. BRITT. OMN. REX. ET. INDIAE IMP. The medal was issued in both silver and bronze and there were twelve bars issued:

NORTH WEST FRONTIER 1908. This was awarded to the Mohmand Field Force, Bazaar Valley Field Force and for service at Landi Kotal and north of Adinazai.

ABOR 1911-12 6th October 1911-20th April 1912. For an expedition against the Abors and the first bar awarded with the second issue medal.

AFGHANISTAN N.W.F. 1919. This bar was awarded for service in a full scale campaign which was literally the third Afghan War. After the awards for the first and second Afghan campaigns it seems strange that the third conflict should be dismissed with a clasp—possibly after World War I it would have been incongruous to strike another medal for a minor war.

WAZIRISTAN 1919-21. The Wazirs hastening for their share of plunder and fighting with the invading Afghans and keeping the pot boiling long after their allies had fled back across the frontier.

MAHSUD 1919-20. The aftermath of the third Afghan war.

MALABAR 1921-22. This was awarded for the suppression of the Moplah Rebellion.

WAZIRISTAN 1921-24. A full scale campaign against the northern and southern Wazirs.

WAZIRISTAN 1925. This was issued to small numbers of R.A.F. personnel and the only bar ever awarded to the R.A.F. exclusive of the other fighting services.

NORTH WEST FRONTIER 1903-31. For operations along the Mohmand border and the first medal of the third issue.

BURMA 1930-31. A series of small actions in Burma lasting fifteen months.

MOHMAND 1933. No British regiments served in this operation.

NORTH WEST FRONTIER 1935. More trouble with the Mohmands.

48. Sudan Medal 1910

Authorised by the Khedive in 1911 to replace the 1897 issue. There was a further issue in 1918 which bore a new date and the cipher of the new Khedive. On the obverse is an Arabic inscription reading ABBAS HILMI THE SECOND and the Mohammedan year 1328. The reverse shows a very fine lion standing with his front paws on a plinth, inscribed SUDAN and in front of the plinth is a trophy of native arms. The background shows the Nile, palm trees and the rising sun. The ribbon, 1.3in wide, has a black watered centre flanked on each side by a thin green stripe and a 5mm wide red stripe.

It was issued unnamed and has sixteen bars, each inscribed in English on the left and Arabic on the right. The bars in chronological order are:

ATWOT February-April 1910; S. KORDO-FAN 1910 10th November-19th December 1910; SUDAN 1912 March 1912; ZERAF 1913-14 December 1913-June 1914; MANDAL March 1914; MIRI April 1915; MONGALLA 1915-16 December 1915-16 December 1915-March 1916; DARFUR 1916 March-23rd May 1916; FASHER 1st September-23rd November 1916; LAU NUER March-May 1917; NYIMA 1917-18 2nd November 1917-February 1918; ATWOT 1st January-26th May 1918; GARJAK NUER December 1919-April 1920; ALIAB DINKA 8th November 1919-May 1920; NYALA 26th September 1921-20th January 1922; DARFUR 26th September-22nd November 1921.

49. 1914 Star

A bronze star with three points, the topmost is replaced by a crown to which is affixed a half-inch diameter ring for suspension; the entire piece is a solid stamping. Across the face of the star are two crossed swords with the points and hilts protruding. In the centre, where the swords cross, is a scroll with the date 1914 thereon and on two small scrolls, one above and one below, are the months AUG and NOV respectively. The scrolls are surrounded by a wide laurel wreath. The reverse is plain and the recipient's number, rank, name and unit are stamped thereon in block capitals.

This star was authorised in April 1917 to be awarded to all those who served in France or Belgium between 5th August and midnight on 22nd/23rd November 1914. Service afloat, in any theatre of war, did not count. In October 1919 a bar was sanctioned to all those who had been under fire in either country between the qualifying dates for the star. This bar is bronze with the inscription 5TH AUG-22ND NOV. 1914 on a frosted ground. Unlike previous clasps it has a small hole in each corner to enable it to be sewn directly on to the ribbon. Those entitled to the bar wear a small silver rosette when only ribbons are worn. The ribbon is red, white and blue, shaded and watered.

50. 1914–1915 Star 5th August 1914–31st December 1915

This star and ribbon, sanctioned in 1918, is identical to the 1914 Star, except that the two smaller scrolls are omitted and the centre scroll bears the dates 1914-15. It was awarded to all who saw service in any theatre of war, including the North West Frontier in 1915, but not to those who only saw service for which the Africa General Service or the Sudan 1910 medal was granted. Recipients of the 1914 Star were not eligible for the 1914-15 Star. The insignia GV appears at the bottom of the wreath.

51. British War Medal 1914–1920

This simple silver medal, once commonly seen in pawnbrokers and jewellers windows, commemorates some of the bloodiest battles, fought under the most ghastly conditions, the world has ever known. Although the award is dated 1914-1918 it was in fact issued for certain operations up to 1920, chiefly postwar mine clearance and service in various parts of Russia.

The obverse has the coinage head of King George V with the legend GEORGIVS V BRITT : OMN : REX ET IND : IMP. On the reverse is St. George on horseback trampling the shield of the Central Powers. Underneath is a skull and crossbones, the symbol of death, and above is the risen sun of victory. Around the upper edge are the dates 1914 and 1918. The suspender does not swivel and the ribbon has a broad orange watered centre flanked on each side by white, black and blue stripes. Over five and a half million of these medals were issued, and just over 100,000 bronze medals were awarded to native Labour Corps. It was issued singly without the Victory medal to certain personnel who did not actually serve in a theatre of war.

No bars were issued, although the subject of battle clasps was considered in 1919 by both a Naval and Military committee. The idea was finally shelved on the ground of cost, but it is interesting that the final Admiralty proposals were approved by H.M. The King and printed in an Admiralty Order in 1920. This gave a substantial list of actions and operations, totalling 49 in all. (My father had worked out that he would have been entitled to seven, including JUTLAND and was most annoyed at the stinginess of the Government.)

52. Mercantile Marine War Medal 1914–1918

This medal was issued, but only in bronze, by the Board of Trade to members of the Merchant Navy who served at least one voyage in a danger zone, or six months at sea in certain named occupations, (i.e. pilot ships and lighthouse vessels). The obverse is similar to the British War Medal. The reverse shows the bows of a merchant steamer ploughing through a heavy sea with a sailing vessel in the background and a sinking U-boat in the right foreground. In the exergue in three lines appears FOR WAR SERVICE MERCANTILE MARINE 1914-1918. The ribbon is watered green and red with a thin white stripe down the centre and the colours are supposed to indicate the port, starboard and steaming lights of a ship. Only the recipient's name appears on the edge in indented block capitals.

53. Victory Medal 1914—1918

This bronze medal was awarded to all who were awarded either of the Stars and, with few exceptions, to recipients of the British War Medal. Men who were mentioned in despatches were allowed to wear a bronze oak leaf on the ribbon. The obverse of the medal shows the winged, standing figure of Victory with a palm branch in her right hand and the reverse carries the inscription THE GREAT WAR FOR CIVILIZATION 1914-1919 surrounded by a wreath. The ribbon is 1.55in wide with a rainbow pattern with the colours merging; from the centre, outwards to each edge, they are red, yellow, green, blue and violet. The ribbon is threaded through a half-inch diameter ring which is held by a small loop sweated to the top of the medal. Naming is in faint, impressed capitals giving the recipient's number, rank, name and unit. But in the case of officers only the rank and name is given.

54. Territorial Force War Medal 1914–1919

This bronze medal was authorised in April 1920 for members of the Territorial Force including nursing sisters who, on or before 30th September 1914, undertook to serve outside the United Kingdom, did so between the outbreak of war and the armistice, and were not eligible for either the 1914 or 1914-15 Star.

The obverse is similar to the British War Medal. On the reverse, following the upper half circle of the piece, are the words TERRITORIAL WAR MEDAL, whilst in the centre, within a laurel wreath, is the inscription FOR VOLUNTARY SERVICE OVERSEAS 1914-19. This is yet another instance where the date shown on a medal has nothing in common with the qualifying date for the award. The ribbon is watered yellow with a green vertical stripe, 4½mm wide, a similar distance from each edge. Naming is in impressed block capitals showing the number, rank, name and unit.

55. Naval General Service Medal 1915–1964

Although the first bar to this medal is dated 1909, the award itself for minor naval operations was not instituted until 1915. In common with the Africa General Service medal, there have been three strikings. The first issue, spanning the first three bars, has on the obverse the head of King George V wearing the uniform of the Admiral of the Fleet with the legend GEORGIVS V BRITT : OMN : REX ET IND : IMP. The second issue, covering the period 1936 to 1952 has the crowned coinage head of King George VI and the legend GEORGIVS VI : BR : OMN : REX ET INDIAE IMP. The third and last bears the crowned bust of Queen Elizabeth II with the legend ELIZABETH II D : G : BR : OMN : REGINA F : D. The reverse is the same in every issue and shows Britannia on two sea horses, her left hand resting on a Union Shield, riding through the waves. The ribbon is white with crimson edges 4½mm wide and a narrow crimson stripe spaced 5½mm away from the inside edge of the outer colour.

Fifteen bars were awarded as follows:

PERSIAN GULF 1909-1914. Awarded for operations against gun-runners, pirates and slavers in the Persian Gulf Area.

IRAZ 1919-20. For service in river gunboats on the Euphrates and Tigris during the Arab Rebellion.

N.W. PERSIA 1920. Issued to two officers and two ratings who served in the Naval Mission.

PALESTINE 1936-1939. Awarded in connection with the 'troubles'.

S.E. ASIA 1945-46. Operations in the Java, Sumatra areas and French Indo-China.

MINESWEEPING 1945-51. Awarded for six months minesweeping in specified waters.

PALESTINE 1945-48. Renewal of the 'troubles'.

YANGTZE 1949. Awarded to personnel of all three services connected with the attack on H.M.S. Amethyst and three other vessels by Chinese communist forces.

BOMB AND MINE CLEARANCE 1945-53. Operations as stated in specified area.

BOMB AND MINE CLEARANCE, MEDITERRANEAN. Self-explanatory.

CYPRUS. Eoka operations 1955-1959.

NEAR EAST. Commemorates the operations on the Suez Canal 1956.

ARABIAN PENINSULAR. 1957-1960.

BRUNEI. Brunei, North Borneo and Sarawak. December 1962.

56. The General Service Medal 1918–1964 (Army and Royal Air Force)

This medal was instituted in 1923 for award with appropriate bars for minor campaigns which did not justify a separate medal (similar to the warrant for the preceding Naval General Service medal).

There are four different issues of this medal, each showing a different obverse. 1. The coinage head of King George V and the legend GEORGIVS V BRITT : OMN: REX ET IND : IMP. 2. The coinage head of King George VI, but wearing a crown and the legend GEORGIVS VI D : G : BR : OMN : REX ET INDIAE IMP. 3. The crowned bust of Queen Elizabeth II and the legend ELIZABETH II D : G : BR : OMN : REGINA F : D, and 4. The same obverse as 3 but a different legend, ELIZABETH II DEI GRATIA REGINA : F : D. The ribbon is purple with a centre green stripe, 10mm wide.

The reverse is similar for each striking and shows the standing figure of Victory holding a laurel wreath over the emblems of the two Services.

The fifteen bars awarded are as follows:

S. PERSIA. Operations near Bushire and Banda Abbas in 1918 and 1919.

KURDISTAN. For peace keeping and skirmishes in 1919 and 1923. The last date is significant as it was the first time troops were air lifted.

IRAQ. An Arab rebellion in Iraq in 1919 and 1920.

N.W. PERSIA. For the North Persia Force in 1920.

SOUTHERN DESERT, IRAQ. For services in the Southern Desert in 1928 and awarded solely to R.A.F. units.

NORTHERN KURDISTAN. For operations in 1932.

PALESTINE. For the troubles in 1936-1939.

S.E. ASIA 1945-46. An interesting bar covering postwar operations in

Java, Sumatra and French Indo-China.

BOMB AND MINE CLEARANCE 1945-49. Self-explanatory and largely for operations in the U.K.

PALESTINE 1945-48. Back to the troubles.

MALAYA. Anti-communist operations in Colony of Singapore from 1948 to 1950 and the Federation of Malaya for two months in 1960.

CYPRUS. For operations from 1955 to 1959.

NEAR EAST. The Suez Canal landings in 1956.

ARABIAN PENINSULAR. For service in the Gulf States, Sultanates of Muscat and Oman and the Colony and Protectorate of Aden from 1957 to 1960.

BRUNEI. For operations in Brunei, North Borneo and Sarawak in December 1962.

57. India General Service Medal 1936–1939

This medal was instituted in 1938 and replaced the 1908 award. There are two different strikings, one from England and the second minted in Calcutta. The latter is slightly thicker and the general finish is poor compared with the English striking. The obverse of the medal shows the crowned coinage head of King George VI and the legend GEORGIVS VI D : G : BR : OMN : REX ET INDIAE IMP. On the reverse is a rather peculiar shaped tiger apparently trying to bite his tail. Above him is the word INDIA and below is rocky ground. The ribbon has a stone colour centre flanked by a thin red stripe on each side and green edges 6mm wide. An ornamental suspender and rosettes of typical India medal pattern. Naming is in thin impressed capitals. There are two bars: NORTH WEST FRONTIER 1936-37 and NORTH WEST FRONTIER 1937-1939.

58. 1939–1945 Star (3rd September 1939–15th August 1945)

Although the second World War officially ended on 2nd September 1945 active operations against Japan ceased on 15th August 1945. The qualifications for this award were as follows: for the Royal Navy six months service afloat in areas of active operations were required. For the Army six months service in an operational command were required, but only one days service in Dunkirk, Norway and certain specified commando raids. Airborne troops qualified for the star on participating in an airborne operation provided they had completed two months service in an operational unit. The R.A.F. qualified for the award for any flying operations against the enemy, provided that two months service had been completed in operational units; ground crew had to complete six months service in the area of an operational command except for Dunkirk and Norway. For Merchant Navy personnel qualified for six months service afloat with at least one voyage through specified 'dangerous waters'–the latter including service during the evacuation from Dunkirk. Irrespective of the six months qualification period, all service personnel qualified once they were decorated or mentioned in despatches, killed in action or died on service, evacuated as the result of wounds or sickness on service, or were evacuated from Dunkirk, Norway, Crete and Greece. The time spent as a prisoner of war also counted. Air crews of fighter aircraft engaged in the Battle of Britain between 10th July and 31st October 1940 were awarded a bar inscribed BATTLE OF BRITAIN. A silver-gilt rose emblem takes the place of the bar when only a ribbon is worn, and this applied to all other bars issued for World War II.

In common with the remaining campaign stars, the 1939-45 award is a six-pointed bronze star with a ring, embodied at the head of the top point, which holds the suspension ring. In the centre is the Royal Cypher surmounted by a crown. The latter is superimposed on a circlet which bears the title of the star. The reverse is plain and unnamed (a penny pinching decision which reduced the value of the award to both the recipient and subsequent collectors). The ribbon has three equal stripes of dark blue, red and light blue, representing the services.

59. The Atlantic Star 3rd September 1939—8th May 1945

This award was granted for six months
service afloat in the Atlantic, Home
Waters, convoys to Russia or certain parts
of the South Atlantic. Personnel of the
Royal Navy qualified provided they had
first earned the 1939-1945 Star for six
months service in an operational area and,
with minor differences, the same held for
men of the Merchant Navy. Air crews
qualified for any operation against the
enemy in the specified areas, provided
they had two months service in an operational unit, and the prior award of the
1939-45 Star. Army and R.A.F. personnel
serving with the Royal or Merchant Navy
qualified in the same way as members of
the service to which they were attached.
Those who were not able to complete the
qualifying period and were not eligible for
the 1939-45 Star were awarded the
Atlantic Star. In common with the other
campaign stars, any length of service
terminated by death or disability, or
where the recipient was decorated or
mentioned in despatches, also qualified.
Two bars were issued, AIR CREW
EUROPE and FRANCE AND
GERMANY, but not more than one could
be earned by any one man. The ribbon is
shaded and watered blue, white and sea
green.

60. The Air Crew Europe Star 3rd September 1939—5th June 1944

This star, the rarest of the World War II
stars was awarded for operational flying
from United Kingdom bases over Europe
(including the United Kingdom) for two
months. Service in operations at sea did
not count. Two bars were issued
ATLANTIC or FRANCE AND
GERMANY. The ribbon is pale blue
flanked by a narrow black stripe on each
side and black edges, symbolizing the
continuous day and night flying of the
R.A.F. This is also one of the stars which
have been copied. There are a number of
differences, but the most striking is the
fact that in the Royal Cypher, the top of
the V and I are joined in the original, but
separated in the copy.

61.   The Africa Star 10th June 1940–12th May 1942

The qualification for this Star was one or more days service in (or in the case of the R.A.F. over) North Africa between 10th June 1940 and 12th May 1943, or Abyssina, Italian Somaliland, Sudan, Eritrea and Malta. Royal or Merchant Navy service anywhere at sea in the Mediterranean also qualified.

Three bars were awarded which consisted of: 1. 8TH ARMY for service in the Eighth Army between 23rd October 1942 and 12th May 1943. 2. 1ST ARMY for service in the First Army, or any unit under the command of that army from 31st December 1942 to 12th May 1943 and 3. NORTH AFRICA 1942-43 to Naval, R.A.F. and Merchant Navy personnel operating in specified areas from 23rd October 1942 to 12th May 1943.

When only ribbons are worn these clasps are replaced by 1, the arabic numeral '8'; 2, the arabic numeral '1'; and 3, a small silver rosette. During the same dates inshore service by the Merchant Navy, certain commands of the R.A.F. and the personnel of the Headquarters of 18th Army Group earned a silver rose emblem instead of one of the bars. Although an individual might qualify for all three clasps he was only awarded the one to which he was first entitled.

The ribbon is pale buff with a wide red stripe in the centre. Equidistant between the edges of the ribbon and the middle stripe are a thin dark blue stripe on the left and a thin pale blue stripe on the right. The colours represent the services and the sand of the desert.

62.   The Pacific Star 8th December

Naval and R.A.F. crews had to complete at least one operational sortie over certain specified land or sea areas before being eligible for this award. In the case of the Army there was no prior time qualification but only service in the Pacific theatre of operations in territories invaded by Allied or enemy forces. Hence those unfortunates who disembarked at Singapore and were marched straight into Japanese prisoner-of-war camps earned a Pacific Star (and earned it in a very hard way) despite the fact they were never in action.

This is a multi-coloured ribbon with a pale yellow stripe down the middle, flanked by a green stripe on each side, a narrow dark blue stripe on the right, a pale blue narrow stripe on the left and wider red edges. The colours are symbolical of the jungles and beaches of the Pacific and fighting services. There is one bar BURMA.

63. The Burma Star 11th December 1941–2nd September 1945

The Army qualified for this award for operational service in Burma during the whole of the period, in Bengal and Assam between 1st May 1942 and 2nd September 1945. Service in China and Malaya between 16th February 1942 and the last date was also included. R.A.F. air crew qualified with one operational flight over those areas, but ground crew and staff were subject to similar rules as the Army. Awards to the Royal and Merchant Navies were confined to a large area of the Bay of Bengal, including the Malacca Strait.

The ribbon has a broad red central stripe flanked on either side by a blue stripe of similar width. In the centre of each of the blue edges is a narrow orange stripe. One bar PACIFIC was issued with this Star.

1941–2nd September 1945

64.   Italy Star 11th June 1943—8th May 1945

Although termed the Italy Star it was
awarded for active service in Italy, Sicily,
Greece, Yugoslavia, Corsica, Sardinia, Elba
and the Aegean and Dodecanese. However,
service in Sicily after 17th August 1943,
Sardinia after 19th September 1943 and in
Corsica after 4th October 1943 did not
qualify. Generally speaking, entry into
Austrian territory during the closing stages
of the war also qualified. R.A.F. air crew
who took part in operations within the
Mediterranean theatre, including operations over Europe from Mediterranean
bases, also qualified. Conditions for
R.A.F. ground forces and Naval shore
parties were similar to those for army
personnel. The Royal Navy and the
merchant service personnel qualified by
service afloat in and around the areas
mentioned and including operations off
the south of France.

  The ribbon is five equal widths of red,
white, green, white and red, representing
the Italian national colours. There were no
bars for this award, and thus the Italy Star
was also granted in addition to other stars.

---

65.   The France and Germany Star 6th June 1944—8th May 19

This Star was awarded for operational
service in France, Belgium, Holland and
Germany between the dates shown, that is
from D-Day until the German surrender.
Royal and Merchant Navy personnel
qualified with service afloat in direct
support of land operations. Air crews were
eligible for service against the enemy over
Europe, except flights which emanated
from the Mediterranean area. Naval
landing parties and non-aircrew personnel
qualified under the same conditions as the
Army.

  The colours of the ribbon are blue,
white, red, white and blue in equal widths
and represent the colours of the Union
Jack, France and the Netherlands. There
was one bar ATLANTIC. In common with
the other campaign stars which also
carried bars, a recipient was only awarded
the star for which he first qualified, plus
one bar for further service. There was no
AIR CREW EUROPE clasp.

66. The Defence Medal 3rd September 1939—15th August 1945

This cupro-nickel medal has the coinage head of King George VI with the usual legend on the obverse. The reverse shows the Royal Crown resting above a small oak tree and flanked by two heraldic lions. The dates 1939 and 1945 appear in the top left and right respectively, whilst beneath the design are the words THE DEFENCE MEDAL. The ribbon is flame coloured with green edges and symbolises the air attacks and destruction on our green land. The nationwide black-out is represented by a narrow black stripe down the centre of each of the green edges. Generally speaking, this medal was awarded for three years service in Great Britain until 8th May 1945 or six months overseas in territories subjected to, or threatened by enemy attacks. The time was extended to forces overseas until 15th August 1945, the end of the war in the Pacific. In the case of mine and bomb disposal units the time qualification was three months.

Owing to the terms of reference for campaign awards it is not unusual to find a man with several stars who has never heard a shot fired in anger. Conversely, a man with only the Defence Medal who earned it, for example, whilst serving with the fire or rescue services in London or any other city subjected to constant air attack, wears a medal worth having. In common with all other decorations and medals only the man who wears the medal knows how it was earned.

67. The War Medal 3rd September 1939–2nd September 1945

This medal is also cupro-nickel and on the obverse has the crowned head of King George VI with the usual legend. On the reverse is a British Lion standing over a vanquished dragon. The dates 1939 and 1945 appear in two lines in the top right. The ribbon embodies the colours of the Union Jack and is red, blue, white, blue and red in equal widths. A thin red stripe runs down the centre of the white portion. It was awarded to all full time personnel of the armed forces who completed twenty-eight days service during the qualifying dates. For merchant seamen there was a separate requirement, that the twenty-eight days must have been served at sea. Service terminated by death, wounds or capture also qualified. Thus a man taken prisoner at Dunkirk has two ribbons to show for his five years' captivity, the 1939-45 Star and the War Medal.

The War Medal ribbon may also carry one bronze oak leaf emblem signifying the wearer has been mentioned in despatches, irrespective of the theatre of war or the number of times mentioned.

69. The Campaign Service Medal

As the three armed services were amalgamated under one ministry, the Ministry of Defence, a new medal was instituted in 1964 for award to all the fighting services.

The obverse (similar to no. 70) carries the crowned effigy of Queen Elizabeth II with the legend ELIZABETH II DEI GRATIA REGINA F:D, and the reverse has the words FOR CAMPAIGN SERVICE surrounded by a laurel wreath. It has an ornamental swivelling suspender, similar to the obsolete General Service

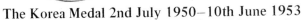

68. The Korea Medal 2nd July 1950—10th June 1953

There are two issues of this medal which differ only in the legend on the obverse. Both show the laureated head of Queen Elizabeth II, but whereas the first type has the wording ELIZABETH II DEI GRA : BRITT : OMN : REGINA F : D:, the second is worded ELIZABETH II DEI. GRATIA. REGINA F:D. One school of thought believes that the second issue is an error, but this is difficult to believe. It is cupro-nickel, but the medal issued by Canada is silver, and has the word CANADA beneath the Queen's head. On the reverse is Hercules, armed with a short sword fighting the many-headed Hydra. In the exergue is the word KOREA. The ribbon has five equal stripes of yellow, blue, yellow, blue and yellow. The naming is impressed in thin capitals.

The medal was sanctioned in 1951 for award to members of the British Commonwealth Forces who fought on behalf of the United Nations on the side of South Korea. One day's service in Korea qualified personnel of any of the three services or twenty-eight days sea service in the operational areas of the Yellow Sea and Sea of Japan for the Royal Navy. R.A.F. personnel qualified either in accordance with the rules for the Navy and Army, or one operational sortie over Korea or Korean waters. Anyone awarded the Korea medal also received the United Nations medal with bar KOREA. This medal is made of bronze alloy and has a very cheap appearance. The ribbon has seventeen alternate vertical stripes of blue and white.

1962 to date

medal, and the ribbon is purple with green edges. Naming is in impressed small block capitals.

Five bars have so far been awarded and they are:

1. BORNEO. Services against the rebels in North Borneo, Sarawak or Brunei from 24th December 1960 until
2. RADFAN. Operations in the South Arabian Federation from 23rd

April to 31st July 1964.
3. SOUTH VIETNAM (awarded only to Australian and New Zealand forces) 24th December 1962-29th May 1964.
4. SOUTH ARABIA. For services in that area from 1st August 1964 to 30th November 1967.
5. MALAY PENINSULAR. 17th August 1964 to 11th August 1966.
6. NORTHERN IRELAND 14th August 1969-

70. The Vietnam Medal 1964—

The terms of the Royal Warrant restrict this award to members of the Australian armed forces serving in Vietnam on or after 29th May 1964. By the same token it is possible for a man to earn both this and the preceding medal in cases where his tour of duty overlaps the qualifying date.

On the obverse of the medal is the crowned effigy of Queen Elizabeth II with the legend ELIZABETH II DEI GRATIA REGINA F.D. . The reverse has a symbolical representation of the idealogical war in Vietnam and depicts a naked man, left hand outstretched, holding back an encroaching sphere. Behind him is another sphere and following the curve of the medal, above his head, the word VIETNAM.

The ribbon is bordered on the left by a dark blue stripe and on the right by a light blue stripe, each 6mm wide. Both blue margins are flanked by a red stripe 3mm wide. The remainder of the ribbon is yellow apart from three vertical equidistant red stripes, each one mm wide and the same distance apart, in the middle. The colours represent the three armed services and blood, against the background of Asia.